SpringerBriefs in Economics

More information about this series at http://www.springer.com/series/8876

Frank P. Jozsa Jr.

National Basketball Association Strategies

Business Expansions, Relocations, and Mergers

Springer

Frank P. Jozsa Jr.
Tega Cay, SC, USA

ISSN 2191-5504 ISSN 2191-5512 (electronic)
ISBN 978-3-319-10057-9 ISBN 978-3-319-10058-6 (eBook)
DOI 10.1007/978-3-319-10058-6
Springer Cham Heidelberg New York Dordrecht London

Library of Congress Control Number: 2014949261

Printed on acid-free paper

Springer is part of Springer Science+Business Media (www.springer.com)

To Pfeiffer University Library
Director Lara Little

Acknowledgements

To research topics and then organize, write, and edit a manuscript of *National Basketball Association Strategies*, I received expert advice, encouragement, and other types of assistance from the following people.

Pfeiffer University Library Director and Assistant Professor of Library Science Lara Little, to whom I dedicated this book, accessed several online databases and forwarded me numerous references including academic studies, articles, book reviews, professional reports, website addresses, and college dissertations and theses. Besides her excellent communication skills, Lara is conscientious, efficient, and smart. She processed my requests for information within 1 or 2 days and never questioned or failed to complete them. Certainly, Lara is an outstanding librarian and library director for Pfeiffer's campuses in Misenheimer and Charlotte, North Carolina.

Employed at the Pro Basketball Hall of Fame, Matt Zeysing told me the facility does not have a general overview of National Basketball Association team histories online or in the museum. For that information, Matt recommended I contact teams on nba.com and/or visit a local library and ask a librarian for a series titled *Team Spirit* (Norwood House Press, 2014) by Mark Stewart. In addition, he recommended for my research recent editions of the *Official NBA Guide* and *Official NBA Register*. Thus, special thanks to Matt for his sources about the league and its teams and their former and current owners, coaches, and players.

I am grateful to Professor Daniel Rascher for forwarding me his views regarding the potential for future expansions and team relocations in the National Basketball Association. Currently, he is Director of Academic Programs for Sport Management Programs at the University of San Francisco.

Besides Lara, Matt, and Daniel, others who helped me with locating and reviewing the literature about professional basketball leagues, teams, and seasons were the University of Michigan Professor Rodney D. Fort, Penn State University Professor Murray R. Nelson, sports author Connie Kirchberg, Orlando Magic Senior Vice President Pat Williams, and librarians at the Fort Mill and York County Public Library in South Carolina. In fact, Professor Fort's online business database contains historical attendances and financial information of teams in each major sports league in America. For sure, I appreciate their assistance.

Since the late 1990s, nursing administrator and educator Dr. Maureen Fogle has provided resources and opportunities for me to continue authoring sports books. Besides sharing an office, she supports me in other ways and knows my history of being a former college baseball and basketball athlete, and a student and economics professor. I sincerely thank Maureen for her patience, tolerance, and love.

Frank P. Jozsa Jr.

Contents

Part II Team Relocations

Part III League Mergers

Chapter 1
Introduction

For demographic, economic, and sports-specific reasons, the 3-year-old Basketball Association of America (BAA) and 12-year-old National Basketball League (NBL) merged and formed another professional organization in 1949. Named the National Basketball Association (NBA), it has become a popular, prosperous, and successful group of franchises. In addition to multiple sports markets across the United States (US) and one in Canada, the league has an enthusiastic, large, and expanding fan base in several foreign countries including China, Italy, and the Philippines.[1]

To operate at sites in cities of metropolitan areas for more than six decades, NBA officials made short- and long-run business decisions that affected in some way the current and future costs, revenues, and profits of teams and also their owners, coaches, and players. The league's clubs struggled during many years because they had to compete with Major League Baseball (MLB) and the National Football League (NFL) and National Hockey League (NHL) for fans to attend their regular season and postseason games and watch them on local, regional, and national television networks. In short, it was crucial for the NBA to anticipate and effectively confront and adapt to these challenges and problems by developing, evaluating, and implementing different, risky, and unique strategies. Indeed, that is the central theme of this book.

[1] NBA games are popular among sports fans in these and other foreign countries. See Benjamin Markovits, "A New Global Game?" *New Statesman* (19 January 2009), 28; David Stone, "Stern Sets His Sights Overseas," *Basketball Digest* (May 2002), 3; "NBA Returning to London for Regular Season Matchup" at http://www.nba.com cited 21 March 2014.

F.P. Jozsa Jr., *National Basketball Association Strategies*,
SpringerBriefs in Economics 84, DOI 10.1007/978-3-319-10058-6_1

Purpose and Objectives

Written for various audiences, the purpose of *National Basketball Association Strategies* is to examine how, when, and why the NBA decided to change, continue to operate, and gradually thrive as an organization from 1949 to 2014. Indeed, this is important business, cultural, and historical information to comprehend, remember, and study especially for prior, current, and potential NBA franchise owners and executives, professional basketball fans in America and those in other nations, and sports economists, historians and researchers. Besides them, others are journalists and reporters in the media, and college and university students enrolled in undergraduate and graduate sports administration, business, and management courses. To that end, following are five key objectives of this book and contents of chapters.

First, *National Basketball Association Strategies* denotes how the league changed in composition, size, and structure. As a result, readers learn when and why the NBA agreed to accept or reject bids from individuals and syndicates of investors to own and operate an expansion franchise in small, midsized, and large markets where, perhaps, there were one or more MLB, NFL, and/or NHL teams.

Second, readers will know that some sports markets in the US and one in Canada opened and then failed to support an NBA team in periods and generations of the twentieth and early twenty-first centuries. Thus, the league expanded and allocated its teams among metropolitan areas in response to the development, growth, and prosperity of local and regional economies.

Third, the book's audiences realize that qualitative factors–besides collective bargaining agreements, revenue sharing, and players' salaries–contributed to the evolution, progress, and wealth of the NBA. These factors include such intangible but personal and important attributes as cooperation, discipline, intuition, leadership, motivation, and optimism.

Fourth, *National Basketball Association Strategies* indicates why different teams in this sport compared to those in professional baseball, football, and ice hockey were able to exist for one or more years or alternatively, failed to entertain and satisfy the demands of sports fans. In other words, some NBA clubs became increasingly popular despite economic recessions, social trends, and military conflicts while others never did appeal to young people and adults.

Fifth, readers will appreciate and understand the influence, role, and consequences of expansion franchises, team relocations, and mergers in NBA history. Since 1949, league officials applied these strategies for new and existing teams to develop, compete and mature, and for their owners to anticipate and react to financial, managerial, and marketing plans made by decision makers in MLB, NFL, and NHL.

Book Reviews

Since the early 1990s, several books document and discuss the history of leagues and teams in professional basketball. Some of them, in part, reveal and analyze the NBA's growth, maturity, and prosperity as a business, and furthermore, provide detailed information and statistics about performances of this league's teams and their coaches and players. Based on publication dates in chronological order, this section summarizes the contents of a few titles because they identify, relate to, and mention sports organizations and other topics in *National Basketball Association Strategies*. For additional sources, the Bibliography contains references to articles and various books, dissertations, Internet readings, and media guides.[2]

In *Pay Dirt*, authors James Quirk and Rodney D. Fort analyze such matters as the distinctive and lucrative features of professional sports facilities, special tax shelters for franchise owners, sports markets of teams, and the problems and failures of rival leagues. According to their research, the most important economic benefit generated by a professional sports team for a city is identification as a symbol, which unifies people within it and the surrounding area's population. However, the immediate and future values of the benefit are difficult to measure in dollars and estimate quantitatively.

Power, prestige, and millions of dollars—these are the stakes in *The Sports Franchise Game*. In this 1995 book, sports attorney Kenneth L. Shropshire describes the franchise warfare that pits city against city in the fierce bidding competition to capture major league teams. Rigorous research, fascinating interviews with major players, stories behind the headlines, and an insider's perspective converge in this view of the business side of professional sports. Author Shropshire portrays a complex web of motivations, negotiations, and public relations, and discusses examples of sports franchises from Philadelphia, the Bay Area, and Washington, DC.

Published by Quorum in 1999, *Relocating Teams and Expanding Leagues in Professional Sports* covered aspects of the NBA and other major leagues from 1950 to the late 1990s. From a business perspective, the book describes the NBA's growth in new markets and movements of existing teams from their sites in cities to metropolitan areas across the US Historical demographic and economic data provide the context. The authors apply metropolitan area statistics, game attendances, and financial values to franchise owners and league decisions, rank the performances of teams, and describe such issues as taxpayer subsidies for new venues and the impact of professional teams on cities and regions.

Hoop Lore traces the origins of basketball and development of the sport's professional leagues. Written by Connie Kirchberg and published in 2007, the book covers the status of the NBA as of the early 2000s and portrays how the league overcame

---

[2] Besides references and sources in the Bibliography, see such websites as baseketball-reference.com, databasebasketball.com, forbes.com, hickoksports.com, hoopedia.nba.com, insidehoops.com, nba.com, rodneyfort.com, sportsbusinessnews.com, sportsencyclopedia.com, and teammarketing.com. Two recent sources for researching historical NBA data are the *Official NBA Guide: 2013–14 Edition* (New York, NY: NBA Properties, 2013), and the *Official NBA Register: 2013–14 Edition* (New York, NY: NBA Properties, 2103). For information about the formation and early history of the NBA, see Frank P. Jozsa Jr. and John J. Guthrie Jr., *Relocating Teams and Expanding Leagues in Professional Sports: How the Major Leagues Respond to Market Conditions* (Westport, CT: Quorum Books, 1999); Connie Kirchberg, *Hoop Love: A History of the National Basketball Association* (Jefferson, NC: McFarland, 2007); Robert W. Peterson, *Cages to Jump Shots: Pro Basketball's Early Years* (New York, NY: Oxford University Press, 1990); Charles Rosen, *The First Tip-Off: The Incredible Story of the Birth of the NBA* (New York, NY: McGraw-Hill, 2008).

obstacles to become one of the most successful brands in professional team sports. If you want to know about multimillion-dollar arenas, players' shoe endorsements, and professional basketball during its inception to the modern era of glory, this title contains that and other historical information.

Published by McFarland in 2009, Murray R. Nelson's *The National Basketball League* is a first history of the league, which held court from the mid-1930s until its merger with the BAA in 1949. Originally formed in Akron and Indianapolis, the league operated mainly in the Midwest but extended as far east as Rochester and Syracuse and west to Denver, building major franchises with hometown loyalties. Most of its best players were college graduates, a major change from previous professional leagues, and it was the first modern major professional league to integrate. The book's features include photographs, maps of league franchises, tables of team standings, and achievements of the league's most valuable players and scoring leaders.

Born in 1967, the American Basketball Association (ABA) had nine tumultuous seasons and introduced fans to such legendary superstars as Julius Erving, Connie Hawkins, George Gervin, and Moses Malone. In *Loose Balls*, former newspaper writer Terry Pluto spins an irreverent history in interview format of the ABA featuring its three-point shot, slam-dunk contest, and the red, white, and blue basketball. The league's saga includes unsettled finances, ever-changing teams, and constant war with the more established NBA. Besides great players, readers meet such franchise owners as Earl Foreman, John Y. Brown, and Charles O. Finley, coaches as Hubie Brown and his brother Larry, Bob Bass, and Slick Leonard, bad boys as Warren Jabali and John Brisker, and dozens of others. Published in 2009, this book is a history laced with humor about a league filled with entertainment, excitement, and fun.

The National Basketball Association discusses the development, growth, and success of the NBA from a business perspective. Covering the late 1940s to 2009, it has chapters on the league's expansions and mergers, team territories and relocations, franchise organizations and operations, basketball arenas and markets, and NBA domestic and international affairs. In short, the book explains when, how, and why the NBA emerged, improved its operations, and survived to become one of the world's most dominant and popular professional sports organizations. Apart from the front matter, there is an Appendix, Selected Bibliography, and Index.

Organization and Structure

In addition to the Acknowledgements, *National Basketball Association Strategies* includes this Introduction as Chap. 1 and seven additional chapters followed by an Appendix, Bibliography, and Index. Most important, Chaps. 2–7 identify and discuss the core contents of the book. Next are summaries of chapters and an overview of the back matter.

Chapters 2 and 3 analyze the history of expansion franchises during periods before and then after the NBA merged with the ABA in 1976. They describe why and when the NBA approved applications from ownership groups and the entry of new teams. If available in the literature, there is information including facts and statistics about expansion clubs' attendances at their home games in addition to how successful they were at winning division and conference titles and league championships. The short- and long-run business implications and effects of expansion by the NBA and the league's admission of new teams are each significant elements in sections of these chapters.[3]

Chapters 4 and 5 reveal characteristics and other highlights about NBA team relocations and their home territories both before and after the leagues merged in 1976. They indicate why and when these clubs moved from one metropolitan area to another in the US and one from a province in Canada. The chapters contain attendances at home games and financial profiles if reported, and the performances of each team for specific regular seasons and postseasons prior to and after they relocated. This discussion, in turn, includes reasons for whether, when, and where these teams moved again, or had to consolidate their operations, or simply folded and disbanded as businesses. Similar to expansion franchises, some commercial aspects of teams' territories and relocations were important to highlight in these chapters' contents.[4]

Chapters 6 and 7 discuss two mergers of national sports organizations. These were the NBL and BAA in 1949 and then 27 years later, the ABA and NBA. Because of this strategy, the NBA had more teams and their games and therefore became a monopolistic and powerful group from an economic perspective. Furthermore, the chapters include business reasons for and consequences of these mergers and their significance for professional basketball and other major sports leagues, specific cities and metropolitan areas, and sports fans and markets across the US and in Toronto, Canada.[5]

---

[3] For the NBA's expansion history, see Frank P. Jozsa Jr., *The National Basketball Association: Business, Organization and Strategy* (Singapore: World Scientific, 2011); Frank P. Jozsa Jr. and John J. Guthrie Jr., *Relocating Teams and Expanding Leagues in Professional Sports: How the Major Leagues Respond to Market Conditions*, 43–66, 101–134; James Quirk and Rodney D. Fort, *Pay Dirt: The Business of Professional Team Sports* (Princeton, NJ: Princeton University Press, 1992); and Kenneth L. Shropshire, *The Sports Franchise Game: Cities in Pursuit of Sports Franchises, Events, Stadiums, and Arenas* (Philadelphia, PA: University of Pennsylvania Press, 1995).

[4] Readings about NBA team relocations and territories regarding the Supersonics from the state of Washington to Oklahoma, see for example "Deal Allows the Sonics to Leave Seattle For Oklahoma City," *New York Times* (3 July 2008), 6; Richard Sandomir, "Sonics Given Approval to Oklahoma," *New York Times* (19 April 2008), 2; "Sonics Bid to Leave Seattle Gets League Nod," *Wall Street Journal* (21 April 2008), A10; "Sonics the Most Likely to Move," *Charlotte Observer* (19 February 2006), 14C.

[5] References for the ABA-NBA merger include Peter Carry, "Meanwhile, Back at the Merge," *Sports Illustrated* (24 May 1971), 68; Frank Deford, "Dribbling on the Verge of the Merger," *Sports Illustrated* (9 August 1971), 42, and "Merger, Madness and Maravich," *Sports Illustrated* (6 April 1970), 28; Bill Rhoden, "ABA Superstars Join the NBA," *Ebony* (January 1977), 88–89.

Chapter 8 identifies and then compares five each domestic and foreign cities as future home sites for NBA expansion franchises and also which current teams in both the league's Eastern and Western Conference are most vulnerable to relocate to another city such as in Las Vegas, Pittsburgh, San Diego, Seattle, and/or St. Louis. As a business strategy, the chapter also highlights the potential for mergers between the NBA and interNBLs and the formation of a European Division with new or existing NBA teams in Barcelona, Berlin, London, Madrid, and Paris.[6]

Regarding the book's back matter, the Appendix contains interesting tables of data, statistics, and other information about the NBL, BAA, ABA, and NBA, and the sports markets and regular season and postseason performances of several former and/or current professional teams. Indeed, these tables supplement and verify specific dates, events, and financial values within sections of one or more chapters. Then, the Bibliography and Index are included so that readers have additional readings, references, and sources to learn more about the NBA and history of the sport and specifically to research topics discussed in chapters of *National Basketball Association Strategies*.

In sum, I wrote this book to be a current, useful, and valuable contribution to the literature regarding the game and sport of professional basketball, and to reveal the NBA's short- and long-run strategies as a business and its 66 years of entertaining fans in America and nations across the world.

[6] In 2004, two researchers examined possible expansion or relocation sites for the NBA using a two-equation system requiring two-stage probit least squares to estimate. The location model forecasts the best cities for an NBA team based on the underlying characteristics of current NBA teams. The results suggest that Louisville, San Diego, Baltimore, St. Louis, and Norfolk appear to be the most promising candidates for relocation or expansion. See Daniel and Heather Rascher, "NBA Expansion and Relocation: A Viability Study of Various Cities," *Journal of Sport Management* (2004), 274–294.

Part I
Expansion Franchises

Chapter 2
Before 1976 Season

After completing its 1960 season, the National Basketball Association (NBA) consisted of teams located in such cities of metropolitan areas in the east as Boston, New York, Philadelphia, and Syracuse, and in the west as Cincinnati, Detroit, Los Angeles, and St. Louis. Given that geographic distribution, NBA officials anticipated and shrewdly recognized that some other domestic markets were available for exploitation as potentially attractive sites for new professional basketball teams. When Major League Baseball (MLB) and the National Football League (NFL) and National Hockey League (NHL) expanded in size, the NBA became more ambitious, businesslike, and risky by gradually invading different sports markets across the United States (US) and two in Canada.[1]

This chapter analyzes when, where, and why NBA officials approved the entry of new franchises into the league from 1960 to 1975 (Table 2.1). Furthermore, it discusses how each of these teams performed as competitors and commercial organizations. To support results, two tables contain historical data and other information about the league's strategy to extend its boundaries and power as an economic cartel.[2]

---

[1] Expansions in MLB, NFL, and NHL are, respectively, covered in Frank P. Jozsa Jr.'s *Major League Baseball Expansions and Relocations: A History, 1876–2008* (Jefferson, NC: McFarland, 2009); *National Football League Strategies: Business Expansions, Relocations, and Mergers* (New York, NY: Springer, 2014); *Hockey Business: NHL Franchises, Markets, and Strategies*, an unpublished manuscript at Pfeiffer University in Misenheimer, North Carolina, 2010.

[2] For the NBA's expansion history, see Frank P. Jozsa Jr., *The National Basketball Association: Business, Organization and Strategy* (Singapore: World Scientific, 2011), 21–33; Frank P. Jozsa Jr. and John J. Guthrie Jr., *Relocating Teams and Expanding Leagues in Professional Sports: How the Major Leagues Respond to Market Conditions* (Westport, CT: Quorum Books, 1999); James Quirk and Rodney D. Fort, *Pay Dirt: The Business of Professional Team Sports* (Princeton, NJ: Princeton University Press, 1992); and Kenneth L. Shropshire, *The Sports Franchise Game: Cities in Pursuit of Sports Franchises, Events, Stadiums, and Arenas* (Philadelphia, PA: University of Pennsylvania Press, 1995).

F.P. Jozsa Jr., *National Basketball Association Strategies*,
SpringerBriefs in Economics 84, DOI 10.1007/978-3-319-10058-6_2

Table 2.1 NBA expansion franchises, teams performances, selected seasons

Year	Team	Seasons	Championships	History
1961	Chicago Packers/Zephyrs	2	0	Moved to Baltimore in 1963
1966	Chicago Bulls	48	21	Current NBA team
1967	San Diego Rockets	4	0	Moved to Houston in 1971
1967	Seattle Supersonics	41	10	Moved to Oklahoma City in 2008
1968	Milwaukee Bucks	46	16	Current NBA team
1968	Phoenix Suns	46	8	Current NBA team
1970	Buffalo Braves	8	0	Moved to San Diego in 1978
1970	Cleveland Cavaliers	44	4	Current NBA team
1970	Portland Trail Blazers	44	8	Current NBA team
1974	New Orleans Jazz	5	0	Moved to Salt Lake City in 1979

Note: The slash (/) indicates change in a team's nickname. Year is the expansion year and these teams' first regular season in the league. Seasons are the number of regular seasons as of the expansion year. Championships include division and conference titles and league championships
Source: "Teams" at http://www.basketball-reference.com cited 5 February 2014, and "NBA Teams Websites" at http://www.nba.com cited 5 February 2014

Expansion Franchises

Chicago Packers/Zephyrs

For an unknown fee, a syndicate led by trucking executive Dave Trager purchased an NBA expansion franchise in 1961. He named it Chicago Packers to identify and promote his meat packing company in the city. Indeed, it was the first new team to join the league in 12 years but not very competitive finishing last in the Western Division (WD) with an awful 18–62 (win–loss) record in the 1961–1962 season. However, first-round draft-pick Walt Bellamy from Indiana University became a star for the team by winning Rookie of the Year and placing second to the Philadelphia Warriors' center Wilt Chamberlin with an impressive 31.6 points-per-game (ppg) average and third in rebounds with 19 per game following Chamberlain and Boston Celtics' center Bill Russell.[3]

As a clever marketing gimmick, the team changed its nickname from Packers to Zephyrs before the league's next season but finished last again at 25–55. After drafting former Purdue University All-American Terry Dischinger, who then won NBA Rookie of the Year with a 25.5 ppg, the Zephyrs had the seed for a solid contender with such back-to-back award winners as Bellamy and Dischinger.

[3] The information about franchise owners and their NBA teams' attendances, coaches, performances, players, regular seasons, and postseasons are in such readings as "Teams" at http://www.basketball-reference.com cited 5 February 2014, "NBA Teams Websites" at http://www.nba.com cited 5 February 2014, and "Rodney Fort's Sports Business Data" at https://sites.google.com cited 5 February 2014.

Chicago basketball fans did not get an opportunity to see improvements in their hometown team. Before the 1963 NBA season, majority owner Trager moved his team from Chicago to Baltimore, Maryland and renamed it the Baltimore Bullets.

Winning only 26 % of its regular season games in two NBA seasons, this Chicago expansion franchise had financial problems because its teams failed to attract spectators to Packers' home games at the 9,000-seat International Amphitheatre in 1961–1962 and Zephyrs' games at the 7,000-seat Chicago Coliseum in 1962–1963. In short, Chicago Packers/Zephyrs teams were major disappointments to their owners, NBA officials, and especially sports fans in the northeast region of Illinois.

Chicago Bulls

For a fee of $1.25 million, the NBA awarded an expansion franchise in 1966 to a syndicate headed by entrepreneur Richard Klein. According to the *Chicago Bulls Encyclopedia*, majority owner Klein was brainstorming nicknames for his new franchise and wanted one that portrayed Chicago's status as the meat capital of the world. He was considering Matadors and Toreadors when his young son exclaimed, "Dad, that's a bunch of bull!"

For its decision, Klein's group nicknamed their team after fighting bulls, which had a relentless attitude and instinct of not quitting. Based in northeast Illinois, the Bulls played their home games at 18,676-seat Chicago Stadium and since 1994, at the 20,917-seat United Center in the league's Central Division (CD) of the Eastern Conference (EC).

Despite ownership changes and generally mediocre performances during the 1960s, 1970s, and 1980s, Bulls teams had tremendous success in the 1990s. In fact, they had one of the NBA's greatest dynasties, winning six NBA championships between 1991 and 1998 including twice with three consecutive titles. Hall of Famers Michael Jordan and Scottie Pippen, and reserve Tony Kukoc, rebounder Dennis Rodman, and Coach Phil Jackson led these teams to their victories.

The Bulls are the only NBA franchise to win multiple championships and never lose an NBA Finals in their history. They won a record 72 games during the league's 1995 season and are the only professional basketball team ever to win 70 games or more in a single season. Many sports experts consider the 1996 Bulls to be one of the greatest teams in the NBA history.

The United Center JV, which is a joint venture between the owners of the Bulls and NHL Chicago Blackhawks, signed a new arena naming rights agreement with United Airlines in December 2013. The agreement, which begins in the 2014 NBA season, is worth about $5 million a year and enables United to continue being the official airline of the United Center, Bulls, and Blackhawks. In addition, United receives advertising and promotional exclusivity in the airline category and logo usage rights for the three entities.

Since the early-to-mid 1990s, the Bulls have been one of the NBA's most profitable and valuable teams thanks to many seasons of league-leading attendance and payroll restraint. Although the Bulls recently increased their payroll and incurred a $3.9 million luxury tax, the team's net worth, profits, and revenue rank among the highest in the league.[4]

San Diego Rockets

For $1.75 million, a syndicate headed by sports icon Robert Breitbard purchased an NBA expansion team in 1967 and named it the San Diego Rockets. Because San Diego was the manufacturing center for Atlas rockets and referred to as a "city of motion," the team's nickname was Rockets. Jack McMahon was the Rockets' first head coach while future hall of famer Pat Riley became the team's first draft pick in 1967. That season the team lost 67 games, which was then an NBA record for losses in a regular season.

After the Rockets won a coin toss against the Baltimore Bullets to determine who would have the first overall pick in the 1968 NBA Draft, San Diego selected University of Houston's Elvin Hayes. In 1969, he led the team to the franchise's first ever playoff appearance. However, the Rockets lost in the WD semifinals to the Atlanta Hawks.

Despite Hall of Fame coach Alex Hannum, the Rockets had a 57–97 record and did not make the playoffs in the next two NBA seasons. In addition, San Diego's sports fans preferred to support MLB's Padres and NFL's Chargers while others in the city participated in such outdoor activities as golf, soccer, and tennis. Thus, the Rockets failed to excite many people located in the Southern California region.

Due to apathetic fans, poor performances in regular seasons, financial problems, and small attendances at Rockets' home games in the city's 14,500-seat Sports Arena, Breitbard sold the team in 1971 to Texas Sports Investments, which was a company led by real estate broker Wayne Puddlestein and banker Billy Goldberg. After acquiring the franchise for $5.6 million and with commercial interests and their money invested in Texas properties, they immediately moved the franchise from San Diego to Houston, Texas where it became the first NBA team in the state. In short, San Diego basketball fans did not support the Rockets because the team had subpar seasons, was not popular, and experienced other problems during four NBA seasons.

Seattle Supersonics

For a fee of $1.75 million paid to the NBA in 1967 by Los Angeles executives San Schulman and Gene Klein, the expansion Seattle Supersonics played in the league's Pacific Division (PD) or Northwest Division (NWD) in various regular seasons

[4]Recent financial data about the Chicago Bulls, Milwaukee Bucks, Phoenix Suns, Cleveland Cavaliers, Portland Trail Blazers, and other NBA franchises were in Kurt Badenhausen, Mike Ozanian, and Christina Settimi, "NBA Team Values: The Business of Basketball" at http://www.forbes.com cited 6 February 2014.

from 1967 to 2008. The owners nicknamed their club "Supersonics" because local manufacturer Boeing Corporation received a multimillion dollar contract from the US government to build a supersonic transport airplane.

During its 41-year history in the league, the Supersonics won six division and three conference titles, and in 1979 an NBA championship. Among the team's greatest players were guards Fred Brown, Gary Payton, Nate McMillan, Lenny Wilkins, and Gus Williams, forwards Shawn Kemp and Spencer Haywood, and center Jack Sikma.

Ackerly Communications Inc.'s Barry Ackerly owned the club when he bought the franchise from Schulman for $21 million in 1984 and then 17 years later, sold it to the Basketball Club of Seattle headed by Starbucks chairperson Howard Schultz. Then during October 2006, the Supersonics were purchased from Schultz by Oklahoma City business executive Clay Bennett.

After Bennett failed to obtain a commitment for public funding to construct a new arena for the Supersonics in the Seattle metropolitan area, he moved the team to Oklahoma City before the 2008 NBA season. This relocation followed a $45 million settlement with the city of Seattle to pay off the team's existing lease at Key Arena in advance of its 2010 expiration. In addition, settlement terms of a lawsuit between the city of Seattle and Clay Bennett's ownership group stipulated that the Supersonics' banners, trophies, and retired jerseys must remain in Seattle; that the nickname, logo, and color scheme were available to any subsequent NBA team; and that the Supersonics and Oklahoma City Thunder share the franchise's history.

Milwaukee Bucks

During the late 1960s, the Chicago Bulls were the only NBA team based in the upper Midwest. As a result, Milwaukee Professional Sports and Services Inc. (aka Milwaukee Pro), which was a company headed by executives Marvin Fishman and Wesley Pavalon, paid $2 million in 1968 to obtain an NBA expansion franchise. Given the hunting tradition in Wisconsin, there was no surprise when "Bucks" became the team's nickname in a local contest. For an animal, fans could have chosen much worse names including skunks, which were among other entries. The Milwaukee Bucks were and are a member of the league's EC and currently play in the CD. After purchasing the franchise from Fishman and Pavalon for an unknown price in 1977, 8 years later Jim Fitzgerald sold it to former US Senator Herb Kohl for $16.5 million.

Since 1968, the Bucks have won thirteen division and two conference titles and a league championship in 1971. During its history, the club's most prominent players include such hall of famers as Kareem Abdul-Jabbar, Oscar Robertson, Bob Lanier, Wayne Embry, Moses Malone, Alex English, and Adrian Dantley.

The Milwaukee metropolitan area is one of the smallest and least profitable basketball markets compared to those that host other NBA teams. Consequently, since the late 1980s, Bucks' owners have not greatly expanded the team's payroll to hire potentially productive-free agents and outstanding but older experienced players.

As a result, since 1986 the club has won only one division title. Recently, the Bucks hired a new coach and when the 2013 NBA season began, had only four players on its roster from the previous season.

The 26-year-old BMO Harris Bradley Center is one of the NBA's oldest arenas and thus owner Herb Kohl wants to replace it. The venue recently had a $3 million renovation including luxury suites and theater boxes, but that was not enough of an investment to compete with the newer venues in the league. Although the team's current lease at the Bradley Center exists until 2017, the Bucks receive a limited portion of the arena's suite, merchandise, and concession revenue.

An average of only 13,000 households watched Bucks games in the 2012–2013 season on Fox Sports Wisconsin, which was the second smallest audience for NBA games behind the Charlotte Bobcats. Consequently, the Bucks will continue to be a small-market team that struggles to win championships and generate an excess amount of gate receipts, merchandise sales, and revenue from television contracts.

Phoenix Suns

Because of the region's hot temperatures and remote location, the NBA was reluctant to put a team in the southwest during the 1950s and early-to-mid 1960s. However, convinced that the region had demographic and economic advantages as of 1968, the league awarded an expansion franchise for a fee of $2 million to an ownership group including entertainer Andy Williams. Indeed, the group convinced NBA officials that Phoenix, Arizona's growing population, households with above-average income, large number of televisions in homes within the metropolitan area, and natural rivalries with the league's Los Angeles Lakers and Clippers were factors that supported a decision to admit a new professional basketball team into the area.

General Manager Jerry Colangelo, who was only 28 years old at the time, settled on a name for his expansion franchise in 1968 using a name-the-team contest. In fact, Colangelo chose "Suns" as a nickname rather than Scorpions, Rattlers, and Thunderbirds, and other suggestions included in the 28,000 entries. One lucky fan won $1,000 and season tickets in the contest, which included such obscure entries as White Wing Doves, Sun Lovers, Poobahs, Dudes, and Cactus Giants.

Playing in the WC, the Phoenix Suns are the only team in the PD not based in California. Since 1992, their home arena has been the US Airways Center, which was formerly the America West Arena. Known as the "Purple Palace," the Center has purple seats, which also is one of the Suns colors.

In 1987, Colangelo resigned from the Chicago Bulls and organized a syndicate. That group purchased the Suns from owner Richard Bloch for approximately $50 million. Then, Colangelo hired Johnny "Red" Kerr as head coach and restructured assignments, tasks, and responsibilities in the front office. After a few years, these changes reinvigorated the organization. The Suns won division and conference titles in the 1993 NBA season and their division again in 1995 and 2005–2007.

At the end of the 2012 season, the Suns franchise had the NBA's fourth-best all-time winning percentage in regular season games at 55 %. In 45 years of performances, they qualified for 29 playoffs, posted 19 seasons of 50 or more wins, made nine trips to their conference finals, and advanced to the NBA Finals in the 1976 and 1993 seasons. Based on these results, the Suns are the most competitive franchise in the league to have never won an NBA championship.

Suns teams had three straight losing seasons since appearing in the WC Finals in 2010. In a recent season, the team bottomed out with its worst record since 1968–1969 and fans tuned out with television ratings off an NBA-worst 68 % on Fox Sports Arizona. In addition, attendance at Suns' home games ranked 23 in the team's first season since 2003–2004 without their point guard Steve Nash.

The franchise recently cut ticket prices with more than one-half of upper deck tickets at just $10 per game. The result was an increase in the season ticket base from 8,500 to roughly 10,000. Therefore, despite previous disappointments in their performances, the competitive, profitable, and somewhat successful Suns will eventually win an NBA championship while operating from the 19,023-seat US Airways Center in downtown Phoenix.

Buffalo Braves

During the 1960s, the NBA expanded by six teams. This trend continued in 1970 when, for a fee of $3.7 million, a syndicate headed by investors Philip Ryan and Peter Crotty became owners of an expansion franchise. For personal and perhaps sport-specific reasons, they based their club in a small market area of western New York and named it the Buffalo Braves. However, despite a passion for professional basketball, within weeks the syndicate sold its new franchise to frozen food company proprietor and theme park owner Paul Snyder for an undisclosed price.

While playing in the league' Atlantic Division (AD), the club's competitiveness gradually improved when it finished fourth in the 1970 NBA season, third 2 years later, and second in the 1973 and 1974 regular seasons. During this period, the Braves' best player was former University of North Carolina All-American Bob McAdoo who led them to three consecutive playoff appearances. Interestingly, various Braves' teams played several of their home games at the Maple Leaf Gardens in Toronto, Ontario with the intent to expand the franchise's fan base and market beyond the Buffalo area into Greater Toronto.

One year after the city of Buffalo filed an injunction in court and successfully blocked the Braves' move to Hollywood, Florida, Snyder sold his franchise for an undisclosed amount to fast food chain entrepreneur John Y. Brown Jr. who previously owned the Kentucky Colonels in the American Basketball Association (ABA). To obtain cash and other players, Brown traded superstar McAdoo to the New York Knicks midway through the NBA's 1976 season.

When ticket sales to Braves' home games plummeted, the local community anticipated that the team would relocate soon to another metropolitan area. After two majority owners of the Boston Celtics swapped their team for the Braves organization in 1978, they moved their club from Buffalo to Southern California and renamed it the San Diego Clippers.

Simply put, Buffalo's NBA franchise did not succeed in its territory from 1970 to 1978 because it failed to entertain local sports fans, win any championships, and overcome economic problems in the city. Moreover, the Braves existed in a market whose primary professional sports teams were the NFL Buffalo Bills and NHL Buffalo Sabres, and later the minor-league baseball Buffalo Bisons.

Cleveland Cavaliers

Although baseball and football were popular team sports among fans in cities of northwestern Ohio during the 1930s and 1940s, the Cleveland area also hosted for a few seasons three professional basketball teams that played in the National Basketball League and one in the Basketball Association of America. Given that history, multimillionaire Nick Mileti's syndicate paid the NBA \$3.7 million in 1970 for an expansion franchise.

In a poll conducted by the *Cleveland Plain-Dealer*, local sports fans voted Cavaliers to be the team's nickname. The other finalists included Jays, Foresters, Towers, and Presidents. The Presidents nickname was presumably an allusion to the fact that seven former US Presidents were born in Ohio, second only to Virginia. Jerry Tomko, who suggested Cavaliers in the contest, wrote, "Cavaliers represent a group of daring fearless men, whose life pact was never surrender, no matter what the odds."

Named Cleveland Cavaliers, the club played at home in the 9,900-seat Cleveland Arena and placed fourth in the EC's CD for four consecutive years. After moving into the 10,000-seat Richfield Coliseum in 1974, the team played even better with its annual attendance doubling to approximately 335,000 or 8,200 per game.

Between the mid-1970s and early 1980s, the Cavaliers franchise had financial problems. As a result, different groups owned and then sold the team. For example, minority owner Louis Mitchell bought Mileti's shares in 1980 while Nationwide Advertising Services founder Ted Stepien acquired a controlling interest in it. As majority owner, Stepien made some questionable decisions that involved hiring and firing coaches and trading players. After realizing a loss of \$7 million during 1980–1982, Stepien sold the team in 1983 to business executives Gordon and George Gund for \$20 million.

In March 2005, billionaire Dan Gilbert became majority owner of the Cavaliers and undertook a complete overhaul of the front office, coaching staff, player personnel, and game presentation. Gilbert, however, received national attention during July 2010 when Ohio native LeBron James announced he was leaving the Cavaliers for the Miami Heat on a highly criticized ESPN television special dubbed "The Decision." Following the special, Gilbert published an open letter in Comic Sans font to Cavaliers' fans in which he strongly criticized when, why, and how James made his announcement.

Later in July, NBA Commissioner David Stern fined Gilbert $100,000 for his remarks in the letter. Though some members of the media questioned Gilbert for his criticism of James, many of the team's fans agreed with his letter and even offered to pay the fine. Instead, Gilbert insisted on donating the amount to charity.

Regarding the team's performances, it had moderate success winning three CD titles and one conference championship in 18 total playoff seasons. However, the departure of superstar LeBron James to the EC's Miami Heat in 2010 was a tremendous loss. In 2011, the Cavaliers drafted high school basketball phenomenon Kyle Irving. Since joining the team, he has won such awards as Rookie of the Year, Rising Stars Challenge Most Valuable Player, and All-Rookie First Team in 2012, and furthermore, Irving became an NBA All-Star and Three-Point Shootout Champion. After James' departure and Irving's accomplishments, the Cavaliers fired General Manager (GM) Chris Grant during February 2014 because the team began the 2013 NBA season with a 16–33 record. Then, the club promoted vice president of basketball operations David Griffin to replace Grant.

After James took his talents to Florida's South Beach, the Cavaliers lost 70 % of their games during three of their following seasons. Even so, the team worked hard to entice fans to its home games with attendances at 20,562-seat Quicken Loans Arena about 80 % of capacity from the league's 2010 to 2012 season.

For the 2013 NBA season, the Cavaliers and Milwaukee Bucks became the first NBA teams to display the names of season ticket holders on the court of their home arenas. For sure, this is an added benefit for members of the Wine and Gold United Club, which the Cavaliers launched in 2012. In addition, during the first month since going on sale, demand for the team's single games of its 2013 season exceeded the prior year's total for the whole year. Unfortunately, the Cavaliers had a subpar performance that season against others in its division and thus did not qualify for the NBA playoffs. In short, if GM Griffin improves the team's roster while head coach Mike Brown leads players like Irving to better performances, then the Cavaliers will again be in a conference playoff and perhaps win a series.

Portland Trail Blazers

During the late 1960s, no major professional sports teams were in Portland, Oregon despite the metropolitan areas' growing middle-class and wealthier population. As a result, a syndicate headed by builder and real estate developer Herman Sarkowsky paid $3.7 million in 1970 to own and operate an expansion franchise in the NBA.

To identify his organization to sports fans, franchise officials announced a name-the-team contest. Of more than 10,000 entries, Pioneers was the most popular but ruled out because nearby Lewis and Clark College was already using that nickname. Another popular entry was Trail Blazers, whose logo supposedly represents five players on one team playing against five players from another team. After officials selected Portland Trail Blazers as its name, the team played home games in the city's

12,888-seat Veterans Memorial Stadium during the 1970–1974 NBA seasons and won roughly one-third of them but finished between third and fifth in the PD.

Due to disappointing performances of his coaches and players and with difficult but different financial problems, Sarkowsky sold his interest in the franchise to minority owner Larry Weinberg in 1975 for an unknown price. Two years later, however, the club had a spectacular season and won an NBA championship. Mostly responsible for the team's success was 7-ft center Bill Walton, forward Maurice Lucas, and crafty head coach Jack Ramsey.

From 1977 to 1995, the Trail Blazers sold out 814 consecutive home games at their arena in Portland. Those ticket sales occurred, for the most part, because the club won division titles in 1978, 1991, and 1992, and conference titles in 1977, 1990, and 1992, and an NBA championship in 1977.

Thirteen years after Weinberg acquired the franchise from Sarkowsky, he sold the club to Microsoft Corporation's co-founder Paul Allen for $70 million. To upgrade the organization, Allen invested more resources and money into his franchise and increased players' payroll. These decisions, however, failed to improve the team's performances against its competitors in the WC's NWD.

Since the late 1990s, the Trail Blazers have won only one division title. During this period, the team was inconsistent from season-to-season and usually lacked a superstar and effective head coach. Nevertheless, because of forward/center LaMarcus Aldridge and guard Damian Lillard, the team became competitive in the 2013–2014 and 2014–2015 NBA seasons. If Aldridge and Lillard remain healthy, reserve players score more points, and head coach Terry Stotts makes good decisions, the Trail Blazers will be an excellent team in its division.

Regarding recent business opportunities and their arena, the Trail Blazers' 195 home-game sellout streak ended in March 2013 as the team missed the playoffs for a second straight year. Although it finished with the NBA's fourth highest attendance at 19,829 per game, the team's luxury suite sales were a problem with only 30 of 57 all-event suites leased for the season.

In August 2013, the Trail Blazers added Moda Health as a naming rights partner in a 10-year, $40 million deal. The agreement left only three NBA venues without a corporate name. These include the Detroit Piston's Palace of Auburn Hills, New Orleans Pelicans' New Orleans Arena, and New York Knicks' Madison Square Garden.

Although Allen still owns the franchise, he needs to make more risky, significant, and profitable business decisions for the Trail Blazers to compete against and consistently defeat such opponents as the Oklahoma City Thunder and Denver Nuggets. Otherwise, the team will be mediocre in its division.

New Orleans Jazz

Four years after the Braves, Cavaliers, and Trail Blazers joined the NBA, the league expanded again when it approved the entry of a new franchise for $6.15 million to a syndicate led by Fred Rosenfeld and restaurant entrepreneur San Battisone Jr.

Originally chosen through a name-the-team contest, which produced seven other finalists including Dukes, Crescents, Pilots, Cajuns, Blues, Deltas, and Knights, the team's name became New Orleans Jazz.

Playing at home in the 6,500-seat Loyola Field House for 1 year and then another four in the city's 74,452-seat Louisiana Superdome, the Jazz won approximately 40 % of their total regular season games and finished between fourth and sixth in the league's CD. Meanwhile, the team averaged about 410,000 per season in home attendance. That was because fans loved to watch and especially support a very talented Jazz player. Acquired from the Atlanta Hawks, shooting guard Pete Maravich was popular and usually scored many points each game. During games, he passed basketballs to his teammates like a magician but off the court struggled emotionally and physically with knee injuries, alcohol, and psychological problems.

Besides Maravich's age and deteriorating health, the franchise had issues with its lease at the Superdome. Because of events at Mardi Gras, for example, the Jazz had to play road games for 1 month during the 1977 NBA season while attempting to compete and qualify for the playoffs. In addition, the franchise bungled the rights to draft Michigan State University All-American guard Magic Johnson in 1979, who years later, won several NBA championships with the Los Angeles Lakers.

Demoralized from $5 million or more in financial losses and declining attendances at the team's home games in the Superdome, majority owner Battisone received approval from the league to move the Jazz from New Orleans to Salt Lake City, Utah in 1979. Twenty-three years later, the Louisiana city became home of the New Orleans Hornets (renamed Pelicans in 2013).

Individually, the ten NBA expansion teams had mixed results during their initial five seasons–but only two for the Packers/Zephyrs and four for the Rockets. Ranked accordingly, the Jazz, Braves, and Bucks had the highest average home attendances in regular seasons while the fewest number of spectators were at home games of the Packers/Zephyrs, Cavaliers, and Rockets.

For their average winning percentages, the Bucks, Suns, and Bulls ranked highest but with the lowest percentages were the Packers/Zephyrs, Trail Blazers, and Cavaliers. These results suggest that the Milwaukee Bucks and Chicago Packers/Zephyrs were, respectively, the most and least successful teams within 5 years after they joined the NBA.

From an article in *Forbes* magazine, there is financial information as of 2013 about such original NBA expansion franchises as the Bulls, Bucks, Suns, Cavaliers, and Trail Blazers (Table 2.2). For those teams that moved to another metropolitan area but currently exist, the table contains their estimated market value, revenue, and operating income. Unlike some expansion franchises in MLB and the NFL and NHL, the NBA teams established from 1961 to 1974 did not later disband, fold their operations, or become property of the league.

In 2013, the group of current teams in the table had an average estimated market value of $602 million, revenue of $144 million, and operating income of $26 million. The richest of them were the Bulls and Rockets while the least valuable included the Bucks and Wizards. For the others, their values ranged from the Thunders' $590 million to Cavaliers' $515 million, revenues from the Cavaliers' $145 million to

Table 2.2 NBA expansion franchises before 1976, teams 2013 financial data

Franchises		Current team		
Expansion team	Current team	Value	Revenue	Operating income
Chicago Packers	Washington Wizards	485	122	7
Chicago Bulls	Chicago Bulls	1,000	195	52
San Diego Rockets	Houston Rockets	775	191	63
Seattle Supersonics	Oklahoma City Thunder	590	144	33
Milwaukee Bucks	Milwaukee Bucks	405	109	11
Phoenix Suns	Phoenix Suns	565	137	28
Buffalo Braves	Los Angeles Clippers	575	128	15
Cleveland Cavaliers	Cleveland Cavaliers	515	145	10
Portland Trail Blazers	Portland Trail Blazers	587	140	30
New Orleans Jazz	Utah Jazz	525	131	17

Note: NBA is National Basketball Association. Value is teams' estimated market value in millions based on their current arena deal without deduction for debt (other than arena debt). Revenue is teams' net of arena revenue in millions used for debt payments as of the 2012–2013 NBA season. Operating Income is teams' earnings before interest, taxes, depreciation, and amortization in millions as of the 2012–2013 NBA season

Source: Kurt Badenhausen, Mike Ozanian, and Christina Settimi, "NBA Team Values: The Business of Basketball" at http://www.forbes.com cited 6 February 2014

Clippers' $128 million, and operating income from the Thunders' $33 million to Cavaliers' $10 million. In short, Table 2.2 denotes differences in financial data of ten NBA teams in small, midsized, or large sports markets.

In the Appendix are Table A2.1, which reflects each expansion teams' performance and average home attendance during its first season in the league, and Table A2.2, which lists these teams' city and metropolitan area populations and their population ranks in the expansion year. Table A2.1 denotes that, on average, these ten teams won 26 % of their games, ranked fifth and finished 30 games behind the division leader, had 5,280 spectators at each of their home games, and scored 108 points to their opponents' 115.

Among the group in games, the Chicago Bulls and Portland Trail Blazers had the best records, Milwaukee Bucks and Phoenix Suns ranked lowest in their division, Seattle Supersonics and Portland Trail Blazers attracted the most fans, and the Cleveland Cavaliers scored fewest points and San Diego Rockets the highest. Based on data in the table, the most successful expansion teams in their first season were the Chicago Bulls, Portland Trail Blazers, and despite their rank, the Milwaukee Bucks. Alternatively, the least competitive were the San Diego Rockets, Cleveland Cavaliers, and Phoenix Suns.

According to Table A2.2, Chicago and its metropolitan area had the largest population and ranked highest among NBA expansion teams. In contrast, relatively small markets included Buffalo, Phoenix, and Portland. Despite population differences, the Zephyrs moved from Chicago in 1963, Rockets from San Diego in 1971, Supersonics from Seattle in 2008, Braves from Buffalo in 1978, and the Jazz from

New Orleans in 1979. Thus, 5 or 50 % of the league's initial group of expansion teams remained at their sites through the 2013–2014 regular season.

Before 1976, the NBA experienced some major developments especially its size. In 1950, the league had 17 franchises but quickly regressed to 11 and then a low of 8 in the 1955–1956 season. The largest change occurred from 1966 to 1968 when five new franchises joined the league. Consequently, the NBA increased in size from 8 to 18 franchises in 20 years or in 14 years if you count from when the first expansion team started to play.[5]

[5] An early study of NBA expansion teams appears in Frank P. Jozsa Jr., "An Economic Analysis of Franchise Relocation and League Expansion in Professional Team Sports, 1950–1975," Ph.D. diss., Georgia State University, 1977. Other sources with information are online such as "Basketball History" at http://www.history-of-basketball.com cited 20 September 2005; "History of Basketball" at http://www.library.think.quest.org cited 24 August 2009; "National Basketball Association (NBA) History" at http://www.rauzulustreet.com cited 12 August 2005; "NBA Growth Timetable" at http://www.basketball.com cited 17 September 2005; "Professional Basketball Leagues" at http://apbr.org cited 27 August 2009. Current literature includes the *Official NBA Guide*: *2013–14 Edition* (New York, NY: NBA Properties, 2013), and *Official NBA Register*: *2013–14 Edition* (New York, NY: NBA Properties, 2013).

Chapter 3
From 1976 Season

Between 1949 and 1975, National Basketball Association (NBA) officials approved the entry of ten expansion franchises into the league. Two of these professional sports enterprises had sites in Chicago, Illinois while the others were at home in cities of metropolitan areas within eight different States. As NBA teams, five of them moved elsewhere from their original homes since the expansion year and the other five continued to perform in regular season and perhaps postseason games in the NBA's 2013–2014 season.[1]

During the basketball season before merging with the American Basketball Association (ABA) in 1976, the distribution of 18 NBA teams consisted of six in metropolitan areas of the Midwest, five in the west, four in the east, two in the southwest, and one in the southeast. After admitting four ABA teams into the league totaling 22, there were seven in the Midwest, six in the west, five in the east, three in the southwest, and one in the southeast.

Because of the merger, another team each played in the NBA's Eastern Conference's (EC) Atlantic Division (AD) and Central Division (CD), and two in the Western Conference's (WC) Midwest Division (MD) for a total of 11 in each conference. Alternatively, the remaining six ABA teams folded their operations and disbanded in 1975–1976 or shortly thereafter.

This chapter analyzes when, where, and why NBA officials admitted eight new franchises into the league in years from 1980 to 2004 (Table 3.1). Furthermore, Chap. 3 discusses how each of these teams performed as competitors and commercial organizations. To support results, two tables each in the chapter and Appendix

[1]As denoted in Chap. 2's Table 2.1, the Zephyrs moved from Chicago to Baltimore in 1963, Rockets from San Diego to Houston in 1971, Supersonics from Seattle to Oklahoma City in 2008, Braves from Buffalo to San Diego in 1978, and the Jazz from New Orleans to Salt Lake City in 1979.

F.P. Jozsa Jr., *National Basketball Association Strategies*,
SpringerBriefs in Economics 84, DOI 10.1007/978-3-319-10058-6_3

Table 3.1 NBA expansion franchises, teams performances, selected seasons

Year	Team	Seasons	Championships	History
1980	Dallas Mavericks	34	6	Current NBA team
1988	Charlotte Hornets	16	0	Moved to New Orleans in 2004
1988	Miami Heat	26	19	Current NBA team
1989	Orlando Magic	25	7	Current NBA team
1989	Minnesota Timberwolves	25	1	Current NBA team
1995	Toronto Raptors	19	2	Current NBA team
1995	Vancouver Grizzlies	6	0	Moved to Memphis in 2001
2004	Charlotte Bobcats	10	0	Current NBA team

Note: Year is the expansion year and these teams' first regular season in the league. Seasons are the number of regular seasons as of the expansion year. Championships include division and conference titles and league championships
Source: "Teams" at http://www.basketball-reference.com cited 5 February 2014, and "NBA Teams Websites" at http://www.nba.com cited 5 February 2014

contain historical data and other information about the NBA's strategy, in part, to extend its market and power, prestige, and reputation as an economic cartel.[2]

Expansion Franchises

Dallas Mavericks

Since the National Football League (NFL) Dallas Cowboys and Major League Baseball (MLB) Texas Rangers were the only elite professional sports teams in the Dallas-Fort Worth-Arlington area in 1980, a syndicate headed by Texas entrepreneur Don Carter acquired an NBA expansion franchise for $12 million and played its first season in 1980–1981. These owners nicknamed their team "Mavericks" based on a character in a 1957–1962 western television drama titled *Maverick*.

While playing their home games in Dallas' 17,007-seat Reunion Arena, the team was moderately popular in attendance by averaging 12,000 spectators per game during its first five seasons despite a winning percentage of only 41 %. In 1987, the Mavericks won their first division title and 19 years later a WC championship but then lost in the NBA Finals to the EC's Miami Heat.

[2]For the NBA's expansion history, see Frank P. Jozsa Jr., *The National Basketball Association: Business, Organization and Strategy* (Singapore: World Scientific, 2011), 37–49; Frank P. Jozsa Jr. and John J. Guthrie Jr., *Relocating Teams and Expanding Leagues in Professional Sports: How the Major Leagues Respond to Market Conditions* (Westport, CT: Quorum Books, 1999), James Quirk and Rodney D. Fort, *Pay Dirt: The Business of Professional Team Sports* (Princeton, NJ: Princeton University Press, 1992), and Kenneth L. Shropshire, *The Sports Franchise Game: Cities in Pursuit of Sports Franchises, Events, Stadiums, and Arenas* (Philadelphia, PA: University of Pennsylvania Press, 1995).

Led by guard Jason Terry and forward/center Dirk Nowitzki, the Mavericks defeated the Miami Heat and won an NBA championship in 2011. After the victory, an emotional Nowitzki rushed back to the locker room for some time to himself as the team celebrated on the floor. As a gesture of friendship and goodwill, Mavericks' franchise owner Mark Cuban invited Carter, who still had a 4 % share of the team, on the stage for the trophy presentation. Later, Cuban and his coaches and players lit up the South Beach nightlife displaying their trophy while Nowitzki became the NBA Finals' Most Valuable Player (MVP).[3]

In 2013, the Mavericks missed the playoffs for the first time since 2000, but were still one of only six NBA teams to sell out every regular season game. Owner Cuban kept his payroll in check after totaling more than $100 million in luxury tax payments during the previous 8 years. Although he tried to sign an elite free agent from another team after recent seasons to pair with the NBA's 2007 MVP Nowitzki, these players refused Cuban's offer. In the final year of his contract, Nowitzki earned $22.7 million, which was second highest in the league following Los Angeles Lakers' Kobe Bryant.

Charlotte Hornets

For years, amateur and professional basketball has been popular sports in North Carolina's south-southwest region. After the NBA announced plans to expand by four teams sometime during 1988–1989, millionaire George Shinn organized a group to bid for a franchise. Because of the city's 24,000-seat state-of-the-art Charlotte Coliseum and other reasons, NBA officials awarded Shinn an expansion franchise for a fee of $32.5 million before the league's 1988–1989 season.

In a name-the-team contest, "Hornets" received the most votes. That nickname's origin came from Charlotte's fierce resistance to British occupation during the Revolutionary War when Lord General Cornwallis referred to the city as a veritable "nest of hornets." In addition, some local minor league baseball teams had the name in the early-to-mid 1900s.

During the late 1980s to 1990s, the club was popular initially selling 15,000 regular season tickets and eventually 21,000 of them to Hornets fans. In fact, the Coliseum sold out for 350 consecutive home games. This suggests the franchise earned average-to-large amounts of revenue from gate receipts and such other sources as advertising, concession and merchandise sales, and broadcasting their games on television and radio networks.

---

[3] With his aggressive but sometimes outrageous behavior before, during, and after home games, Mark Cuban's positive attitude inspires the Mavericks to perform above expectations. The league's former commissioner, David Stern, fined him millions of dollars for acting immature, arguing with referees, and interfering in games. Despite his antics, personality, and showmanship, the Mavericks are competitive most seasons among teams in their division.

Because Shinn did not increase his club's payroll enough to retain some star players, the team's failure to win a division title, a tragic accident and death of a player, and embarrassing and immoral allegations involving Shinn, the Hornets' popularity gradually declined and so did its image, reputation, and fan support. Subsequently, Shinn and co-owner Ray Woolridge moved their team from Charlotte to New Orleans, Louisiana in 2002 where it became the New Orleans Hornets.

In retrospect, the NBA made a prudent and rational decision to place a team in Charlotte. The metropolitan area had a relatively large sports fan base plus a huge basketball arena. Despite the team's mediocre performances and public relations problems, it was failure of a public referendum to replace the Coliseum that ultimately caused the relocation of the franchise from Charlotte to New Orleans.

Miami Heat

For decades, southeast Florida was home to professional sports teams including the ABA Floridians from the late 1960s to early 1970s. In 1988, NBA officials awarded an expansion franchise for $32.5 million to a syndicate headed by Carnival Cruise Lines founder Ted Arison. The league's decision was due, for the most part, to Arison's commitment, success, and wealth, to the Miami area's increasingly Hispanic, affluent, and substantial population, and to the city's publicly financed basketball arena.

Named for the region's warm temperature and balmy weather conditions, the NBA Miami Heat played its games before 15,000 or less spectators until the mid-1990s when Arison hired head coach Pat Riley. With Riley's leadership and after trading some veteran players in exchange for talented free agents, the Heat improved its regular season and postseason performances. From the 1992–2013 season, the club competed in 18 playoffs, won 11 division and 5 conference titles, and NBA championships in 2006, 2012, and 2013.

In the 1990s, such players as Alonzo Mourning, Gary Payton, and Tim Hardaway excelled at scoring points and on defense for the Heat. Besides center Shaquille O'Neal, the team was even better during the 2000s with head coach Erik Spoelstra and superstars Dwyane Wade, LeBron James, and Chris Bosh. Although Wade and Bosh are older and sometimes injured, they have the talent to excel and win one or more championships for the Heat.

Because of the Heat's large fan base in local, regional, and national sports markets, the franchise's cash flow, revenue, and profit are among the highest in the league. Within a few years, one or more key players will leave the team. If that occurs, Arison and Spoelstra must replace them with similar talent. Otherwise, the Heat will finish fourth or worse in its division and perhaps out-of-the-playoffs for years.

From a business perspective, the fortunes on and off the court continue to soar for the Heat especially since the arrival of James as a free agent in 2010. Besides winning championships, the Heat's television ratings on the Sun Sports network recently surged 43 % and were the second highest in the league. In addition, the franchise locked up more than one-half of its season ticket holders in a unique 3-year ticket renewal option.

The team's improvements generated a revenue-sharing check for its property owner, Miami-Dade County, for the first time since the arena opened in 1999. The Heat paid for construction of the American Airlines Arena on county-owned land in exchange for a $6.5 million annual subsidy and the promise to share its profits with the county once they topped $14 million. After the team's third championship season since the arena opened in 1999, the Heat delivered a check to the county of $257,134.

Orlando Magic

Because of the city and area's growing populations, increasing household income levels, and popular tourist attractions during the late 1980s, NBA officials awarded an expansion franchise for $32.5 million before the 1989–1990 season to sports entrepreneurs Jim and Bob Hewitt, and Bill DuPont. Based on thousands of responses in a name-the-team contest, these owners rejected such nicknames as "Juice" and "Tropics" and selected "Magic" based, in part, on Disneyland's Magic Kingdom.

During its initial five seasons in the league, the Magic averaged 15,000 fans per game at the 15,077-seat Orlando Arena (now Amway Arena) but won only 39 % of their games. In 1991, multimillionaire Richard DeVos and his family purchased the franchise for approximately $85 million from the Hewitt's and DuPont.

From 1994 to 2013, the team was in 14 playoffs and won 5 division and 2 conference titles. Such coaches as Brian Hill, Chuck Daly, Doc Rivers, and Stan Van Gundy contributed to the team's success during this period along with players Grant Hill, Penny Hardaway, Shaquille O'Neal, Tracy McGrady, Vince Carter, and Dwight Howard.

The Magic's first season after the trade of all-star center Dwight Howard to the Los Angeles Lakers had mixed results. On the hardwood, the team limped to a last place finish in the Southeast Division with only 20 wins, television ratings on the Fox SportSouth network plummeted 55 %, and its average viewership of 14,000 households was third lowest in the NBA. On the plus side, the Magic set a record for sponsorship revenue with the addition of Chase Bank and regular season ticket sales remained strong at roughly 13,000.

In short, the Magic will not qualify for and then succeed in the conference playoffs until DeVos spends more money to recruit and hire a few outstanding players, and thus upgrades positions on the team's roster. It might be years before the team recovers from losing Dwight Howard and his defensive, scoring, and rebounding skills. If the Magic challenges the Miami Heat or another team for a division title, the franchise's attendances at home games, revenue, and operating income will soar at least for that season and perhaps in the future.

Minnesota Timberwolves

Almost three decades after the Lakers moved from Minneapolis to Los Angeles, NBA officials granted an expansion franchise for $32.5 million to business executives Marv Wolfenson and Harvey Ratner before the league's 1989–1990 season. As a result of a name-the-team contest, the club's nickname became "Timberwolves" since Minnesota contained the largest number of timber wolves among the lower 28 states, or about 1,200 of this species during the late 1980s.

The team played its first season while at home in the cavernous 50,000-seat Metrodome and then shifted to the multiuse 19,000-seat Minneapolis Target Center in 1990. For five consecutive years, the Timberwolves averaged approximately 20,000 fans per game at their arena and that included a league record of more than one million in its 1989–1990 regular season despite winning only about 26 % of total games.

During the mid-1990s, the Timberwolves' attendances declined at home because of their poor performances and local and regional sports fans' support of the NFL Vikings and MLB Twins. When Wolfenson and Ratner failed to sell their basketball franchise to a syndicate in New Orleans, multimillionaire Glen Taylor bought it from them and hired former Boston Celtics all-star Kevin McHale to be general manager.

From 1997 to 2004, the club was in eight playoffs and won a division title in 2004 but lost in the conference finals to the Los Angeles Lakers in six games. Besides MVP Kevin Garnett, the team acquired and played such athletes as Latrell Sprewell, Sam Cassell, and Michael Olowokandi. Meanwhile, Flip Saunders was the Timberwolves' head coach from 1994 to early 2005 but then fired in February 2005 by general manager McHale who replaced him to complete the season.

During 2007, the team traded Garnett to the Boston Celtics. In fact, the Minneapolis area was a relatively small basketball market, which did not provide enough revenue for the Timberwolves to retain Garnett and some of his teammates. As a result, the team had a terrible start in the 2007–2008 NBA season with a 5–34 record. In the season's second half, however, the Timberwolves became slightly more competitive in games as they actually escaped last place and posted a record of 22–60 while finishing fourth in the Northwest Division.

Without all-star forward/center Kevin Love, the club struggles to win a championship. Whether it consistently improves in regular seasons depends mostly on owner Taylor and the leadership of general manager and head coach Rick Adelman. Indeed, it may be a decade before the Timberwolves play well enough to make the playoffs and win another division title.

Regarding the franchise's business prospects, the Minneapolis City Council approved financing in November 2013 for a $97 million renovation of the area's Target Center, which is one of the NBA's oldest venues. For the project, the city is contributing up to $48.5 million while the team spends $43 million and building manager Anschutz Entertainment Group (AEG) $5.5 million to pay the balance. Changes to the arena include redesign of the exterior, additional club areas and meeting spaces, and other amenities.

The Council's agreement extends the team's lease to 2032 with renovations to begin in the summer of 2014. Season ticket sales fell to roughly 8,000 in the 2012–2013 NBA season from around 10,000, in part, because the team eliminated many ticket discounts. In addition, fans are upset after the Timberwolves' nine consecutive seasons out of the playoffs.

Toronto Raptors

Six years after two new teams joined the NBA, the league awarded its 28th expansion franchise for a fee of $125 million to a syndicate headed by Canadian John Bitove. To identify his team, entries from a nationwide contest in Canada included such nicknames as Beavers, Dragons, Hogs, Scorpions, Tarantulas, and Terriers. After evaluating these and other entries, the club chose Raptors because of predatory dinosaurs that terrorized people in the movie Jurassic *Park*.

Before the 1995–1996 NBA season, the franchise hired former Indiana University and Detroit Pistons superstar Isiah Thomas as its executive vice president. Then, Thomas selected his friend Brendan Malone to coach the team, which played in the EC's CD. Meanwhile, the roster consisted of players from an expansion draft held in mid-1995.

After performing their home games for four seasons in downtown Toronto's multipurpose 22,911-seat SkyDome (renamed Rogers Centre in 1995), the Raptors moved from there into the city's 19,800-seat Air Canada Centre in 1999 and continues to play their games in that arena before thousands of basketball fans.

During the club's first five NBA seasons, its average attendance was about 17,300 spectators per game. Although winning percentages were less than 50 %, the Raptors improved in their division from eighth in 1996 to third in 2000 and then won a division title in 2007 while competing in five playoffs from 2000 to 2008. Led by head coaches Lenny Wilkens, Kevin O'Neill, and Sam Mitchell, the team's best players included shooting guard/forward Vince Carter, center/forward Chris Bosh, and playmaker Jose Calderon.

To excel in the EC's AD, Raptors' owners must invest more resources into the organization, and especially recruit and hire productive coaches and players. Otherwise, such rival and competitive teams as the Boston Celtics, Brooklyn Nets, and New York Knicks will dominate the division. Based on results since 2008, it is unlikely the Raptors have the administrative officials, coaches, and players to become an elite team and highly profitable enterprise. In short, Toronto is a difficult sports market for professional basketball because fans there support the MLB Blue Jays and most importantly, the NHL Maple Leafs and Canadian Football League Argonauts.

Maple Leaf Sports and Entertainment, which owns the Raptors, Maple Leafs, and Major League Soccer's Toronto FC franchise, made a publicity splash with the hiring of Tim Leiweke who spent 17 years building AEG into a global sports power. Leiweke has a difficult but immediate challenge to improve the Raptors, who for various reasons, missed the playoffs five straight years and finished last in its division during the 2012–2013 NBA season.

Despite the team's relatively poor performances since 1995, the Raptors finished its 2012–2013 season with the highest attendance since 2008–2009. That achievement included 11 sellouts, also a 4-year high. During September 2013, the Raptors added Grammy-winning hip-hop star Drake as the team's global ambassador. The Canadian born artist brings some cache to a franchise that rarely is in the spotlight. Furthermore, the Raptors snagged the rights to the 2016 NBA All-Star game. According to estimates, hosting that event will have a $100 million economic impact for the city.

Vancouver Grizzlies

Located at a site in the province of British Columbia, this expansion franchise joined the NBA in 1995 with Orca Bay Sports & Entertainment its original owner and then years later, millionaire Michael Heisley. After the franchise had settled a legal dispute with the Royal Canadian Mounted Police–who objected to calling the team Vancouver Mounties–"Grizzlies" became the club's nickname since the grizzly bear is a native animal in the province.

Sharing the 19,200-seat General Motors Place with the NHL Vancouver Canucks, the Grizzlies average attendance for five regular NBA seasons was 14,700 per game. From the 1995 to 2000 season, however, attendance gradually declined because the team won only 20–25 % of its games and finished either sixth or seventh in the league's Midwest Division.

From a business perspective, the franchise had several economic and personnel problems while operating in Vancouver, which was Canada's third largest city and located on the nation's west coast. Some of these issues were unique while others reflected a lack of coordination, cooperation, knowledge, and leadership within the organization.

First, the Grizzlies were not competitive in games and did not meet expectations of the league, other teams and their franchise owners, and especially local fans and sponsors. For example, the team won only 16 % of its games in the 1998–1999 NBA season. Second, for various reasons, the team drafted several players who were not productive and frequently failed to perform together in their games. These athletes, among others, included Shareef Abdur-Rahim, Antonio Daniels, Mike Bibby, and Steve Francis. In fact, Francis was occasionally controversial, dissatisfied, and arrogant, and often embarrassed his teammates by criticizing the franchise in the media.

Third, head coaches Brian Winters, Stu Jackson, Brian Hill, Lionel Hollins, and Sidney Lowe failed to motivate their players and did not successfully encourage or reward them to compete and win games especially at home in General Motors Place. Indeed, Winters and Hill were the only coaches to lead their team more than one season.

Fourth, after NBA teams locked out their players in 1998 and then opened their regular season, attendance at Grizzlies' home games plummeted and that, in part, caused financial losses for its franchise owners. This problem, in turn, convinced majority shareholder Jeff LaQueef to sell his interest in the team. When the NHL's St. Louis Blues owner Bill Laurie tried to purchase the Grizzlies, NBA officials rejected his offer. Instead, the league approved Michael Heisley's bid and his plans to own, operate, and keep the team in Canada.[4]

In short, Vancouver was not suitable or adequately prepared as a sports market to host an NBA expansion franchise from 1995 to 2001. Fans there enthusiastically supported amateur ice hockey teams and the Canucks for decades, but not clubs in other sports. Certainly, the Grizzlies' owners lost millions of dollars on their investment. The sale and relocation of the team in 2001 from Vancouver to another site in Memphis, Tennessee was inevitable and realistically, a necessary, prudent, and smart decision by Heisley after getting approval from the NBA.

Charlotte Bobcats

NBA Commissioner David Stern promised Charlotte, North Carolina a new team after the Hornets moved from the area to New Orleans in 2002. Soon thereafter, league officials awarded the city an expansion franchise to open the 2004–2005 season. Its owner was an investment group led by Black Entertainment Television founder Robert Johnson. In a help-name-the-team public contest, "Bobcats" was the most popular nickname rather than Dragons or Flight. An indigenous predator that roams in forests of North Carolina, the bobcat is a fast, fierce, and wild animal, and similar in nature to Panthers, which is the nickname of the city's NFL team.

During its first five seasons in the league, the team's average attendance at the Charlotte Coliseum and then Charlotte Bobcats Arena (renamed Time Warner Cable Arena in 2009) was 15,000 per game although the Bobcats won only 35 % of them. Despite such players as former University of North Carolina All-American's Raymond Felton and Sean May, center Emeka Okafor, and scorers Gerald Wallace and Stephen Jackson, coaches Bernie Bickerstaff, Sam Vincent, Larry Brown, Paul Silas, and Mike Dunlap collectively had their team in one playoff.

In 2006, Robert Johnson hired hall of famer and former Chicago Bulls superstar Michael Jordan as head of basketball operations. With his office and business operations located in Washington, DC, Johnson rarely attended Bobcats home

[4] Born in 1937, Michael Heisley was an American business executive and former majority owner of the Vancouver Grizzlies and Memphis Grizzlies. He orchestrated the team's move from Vancouver in 2001 after promising to keep the franchise in Canada when he purchased it in 2000. Six years later, he agreed to sell his 70 % controlling stake in the franchise to a consortium including former University of North Carolina player Christian Laettner. After the group missed a deadline for the purchase, Heisley found no bidders willing to meet his $300 million asking price. In 2012, Heisley decided to sell the Grizzlies and step aside from his corporate interests due to advancing age.

games although he paid $300 million for the franchise in 2003. During early 2010, there was news that he decided to sell the team for $175 million to Michael Jordan, allowing Jordan to become the first former NBA player to become majority owner of a franchise.[5]

After his team struggled in its division during the 2010–2012 NBA seasons, Jordan officially announced that the organization submitted an application to change the name of the franchise from Charlotte Bobcats to Charlotte Hornets for the 2014–2015 NBA season, pending a majority vote for approval by the NBA Board of Governors at a meeting in Las Vegas in July 2013. NBA Deputy Commissioner and Chief Operating Officer (now Commissioner) Adam Silver said it requires about 18 months for a team to change its identity, but since the league owned the rights to the Hornets' name, that could speed up the process.

The New Orleans Hornets, meanwhile, had recently changed their name to the New Orleans Pelicans for the 2013–2014 NBA season. Thus, in July 2013, the NBA announced it unanimously approved a decision for the Bobcats to become the Charlotte Hornets. As a result, the team's name, logo, and uniforms will change after the 2013–2014 season.

In a widely expected strategy, the Bobcats adopted a modified version of the original Hornets' teal-purple-white palette when they became the Hornets, with black, gray, and light blue as accents. The team officially unveiled its future logo and identity scheme during halftime of a home game in December 2013. That ceremony featured such former Hornets players as Dell Curry (the Bobcats' television color commentator and father of Golden State Warriors' Stephen Curry), and popular Muggsy Bogues, Rex Chapman, and Kelly Tripucka. In addition, the team started a new marketing campaign, entitled "Buzz City," to hype the Hornets' return of its original nickname. In early 2014, the Bobcats revealed new Charlotte Hornets logo shirts, hats, and gear.

While compiling a dismal 21–61 record in the 2012–2013 NBA season, the Bobcats scored the lowest average television rating and audience size among teams

---

[5] Despite spending at least $300 million for the franchise in 2002 and pledging to invest another $30 million to improve it, Robert Johnson's Charlotte Bobcats lost between $20 million and $30 million per year or a total of $200 million while under his control. After selling the team, he called Charlotte's business community arrogant and incestuous and said the city does not do enough for existing and potential minority-owned companies. Johnson, a self-made billionaire, made his remarks at the Urban Leadership Institute, a gathering of mostly black business people. The group presented him with an award moments before he spoke, though the crowd's reaction was different after he made his comments. According to Johnson, "Charlotte is a very, how would I call it, close-knit, arrogant, sometimes incestuous town. It's close-knit, and if you come to this town, and you look like you're one of those people that might break some glass … it's going to be tough for them to relate to. The thing that concerns me is that I'm just surprised that the city doesn't do more for African-American small businesses. And I don't really understand that." See Cleve Woodson, "Ex-Bobcats Owner Blasts Charlotte" at http://www.wcnc.com cited 23 February 2014. For other aspects of Johnson's investment in an NBA team, see "BET Founder Wins Franchise," *New York Times* (18 December 2002), D3, David Sabino and Mark Bechtel, "Expansion Plan," *Sports Illustrated* (28 June 2004), 32, and Richard Sandomir, "Founder of TV Network Becomes First Black Owner in Major Sports," *New York Times* (19 December 2002), A1.

in the league on Fox's SportSouth network despite owner Jordan pumping millions of dollars into his money-losing franchise for working capital. While the Bobcats were among the top beneficiaries of the NBA's revenue-sharing system in 2012–2013, new head coach Steve Clifford will improve the team's performances in its division primarily because of veteran center Al Jefferson, forward Josh McRoberts, and guard Kemba Walker.

For several years, a group of sports writers at *Forbes* magazine has published different types of financial information about professional sports leagues and their teams. Besides data for the New Orleans Pelicans and Memphis Grizzlies, this information appears in Table 3.2 as of the 2012–2013 NBA season for six other original but active expansion franchises highlighted in this chapter.

As a group, their average estimated market value in 2013 was $541 million, revenue $138 million, and operating income $16 million. Compared to the values of all NBA teams, the Heat ranked 7th, Mavericks 8th, Magic 15th, Raptors 18th, and between 24th and 30th were, respectively, the Grizzlies, Timberwolves, Pelicans, and Bobcats.

Besides the worth of their current arena contract, other things influencing each NBA team's value were attendances and gate receipts at home games, market location, size, and wealth, recent winning percentages in regular seasons and number of division titles and league championships, and cash flows from advertising, merchandise sales, and sponsorships.

In the 2012–2013 NBA season, the eight teams' revenue averaged $138 million and ranged from $188 million or 6th in the league for the Heat to $116 million or 28th for the Bobcats. These amounts were different, in part, because of teams' attendances and ticket prices at their home games, the metropolitan area's population and per

Table 3.2 NBA expansion franchises from 1976, teams 2013 financial data

Franchises		Current team		
Expansion team	Current team	Value	Revenue	Operating income
Dallas Mavericks	Dallas Mavericks	765	162	37
Charlotte Hornets	New Orleans Pelicans	420	116	11
Miami Heat	Miami Heat	770	188	29
Orlando Magic	Orlando Magic	560	139	12
Minnesota Timberwolves	Minnesota Timberwolves	430	116	−2
Toronto Raptors	Toronto Raptors	520	149	28
Vancouver Grizzlies	Memphis Grizzlies	453	126	11
Charlotte Bobcats/ Hornets	Charlotte Bobcats/ Hornets	410	115	7

Note: NBA is National Basketball Association. Value is teams' estimated market value in millions based on their current arena deal without deduction for debt (other than arena debt). Revenue is teams' net of arena revenue in millions used for debt payments as of the 2012–2013 NBA season. Operating Income is teams' earnings before interest, taxes, depreciation, and amortization in millions as of the 2012–2013 NBA season

Source: Kurt Badenhausen, Mike Ozanian, and Christina Settimi, "NBA Team Values: The Business of Basketball" at http://www.forbes.com cited 6 February 2014

capita income, and number of wins in their division. To compare them, the Los Angeles Lakers' revenue ranked first at $295 million and Milwaukee Bucks thirtieth at $109 million.[6]

These eight teams' average operating income or earnings before taxes, interest, depreciation, and amortization was $16 million in 2012–2013. Between the New York Knicks' $96 million and Brooklyn Nets' –$19 million, the Mavericks $37 million ranked 7th in the league and Timberwolves' –$2 million was 27th. Apparently, the Pelicans, Magic, Timberwolves, Grizzlies, and Bobcats each had below-average operating income due to expenditures for their tax payments, interest expense on debts, depreciation of capital assets, and amortization on debts and other obligations.

According to data in the table, the two most and least prosperous teams as of the league's 2012–2013 season were, respectively, the Dallas Mavericks and Miami Heat, and Minnesota Timberwolves and Charlotte Bobcats. Besides outstanding players and coaches, the Mavericks and Heat had winning seasons, lucrative arena deals, above-average attendances at their home games, and thousands of passionate sports fans in their local and regional markets.

In contrast to them, the Timberwolves and Bobcats had losing seasons, failed to entertain fans at their home games, owned inferior local or regional sports television rights, and existed in small-to-midsized professional basketball markets. In short, there were significant differences in financial results between the groups of teams for these and other reasons.

Regarding the eight NBA team expansions that occurred after 1976, the Appendix contains Tables A3.1 and A3.2. As a group, they provide additional information about the performances and home attendances of these teams and population data of their cities and metropolitan areas during the expansion year.

During their first season in the league, the Minnesota Timberwolves, Toronto Raptors, and Charlotte Hornets had the highest winning percentages of the group while the Dallas Mavericks, Miami Heat, and Vancouver Grizzlies each won only 15 games. In their division, the worst ranked was the Toronto Raptors who placed 51 games behind the leading team. Furthermore, home attendances were above 23,000 per game for the Timberwolves, Raptors, and Hornets while the Mavericks attracted less than 8,000 at each of its home games in Dallas. The Orlando Magic, meanwhile, scored the most points at 110 per game but also allowed 119. In short, the data indicate that these eight expansion teams had inferior performances in their first season but three of them were popular among local basketball fans based on attendances at home games.

Although the new Raptors and Mavericks clubs played in the most populated markets, others had sites in small-to-midsized cities or metropolitan areas. In Vancouver, the Grizzlies were a struggling team and despite a population of almost

[6] Regarding NBA teams' metropolitan area populations during their expansion year, the two largest and smallest were, respectively, Toronto at 4.2 million in 1995 and Miami at 3.1 in 1988, and Orlando at 1 million in 1989 and Charlotte at 1.1 million in 1988. For this information, see various editions of *The World Almanac and Book of Facts* and *Census of Canada*.

two million people in the area, had the second lowest attendances among expansion teams at their games. Interestingly, cities of the Heat and Timberwolves ranked much lower in population than did their metropolitan areas. This suggests these teams had many fans, respectively, in the suburbs of Miami and Minneapolis.

Given the data in tables for these post-1976 expansion teams' performances, attendances, and populations, 6 or 75 % of them are current members of the league. After only six seasons, however, the Grizzlies moved from Vancouver to Memphis, Tennessee and in 2002, the Hornets relocated from Charlotte to New Orleans. Simply put, the Grizzlies were an inferior team in a small market while the Hornets had a much larger fan base but did not win enough games to contend for a division title.[7]

[7] Some additional information about these expansion teams is in "Basketball History" at http://www.history-of-basketball.com cited 20 September 2005; "History of Basketball" at http://library.thinkquest.org cited 24 August 2009; "National Basketball Association (NBA) History" at http://www.rauzulusstreet.com cited 12 August 2005; "NBA Growth Timetable" at http://www.basketball.com cited 17 September 2005; "Professional Basketball Leagues" at http://apbr.org cited 22 August 2009. For current literature, see the *Official NBA Guide*: *2013–14 Edition* (New York, NY: NBA Properties, 2013), and *Official NBA Register*: *2013–14 Edition* (New York, NY: NBA Properties, 2013).

Part II
Team Relocations

Chapter 4
Before 1976 Season

Organized and established in 1949, the National Basketball Association (NBA) consisted of teams from the former Basketball Association of America (BAA) and National Basketball League (NBL). Several of the 17 NBA teams had home sites in cities of metropolitan areas with small to very small populations while others played their home games in arenas within midsized and large markets.

As professional sports franchises, their economic objective was to earn enough revenue from primarily their ticket sales to generate a profit, otherwise, to break even or unfortunately experience an operating loss. In other words, there was proportionately little income for them then from such sources as television and radio broadcasts, marketing campaigns, partnerships and sponsorships, and the sale of basketball memorabilia and merchandize.

To reveal how NBA teams changed as competitors and sports enterprises geographically and from a business perspective, this chapter analyzes when, where, and why 13 teams moved during 1949–1975 from sites in various cities of metropolitan areas to others and existed there or relocated again. As such, the contents identify each of these organizations and provide reasons they moved and became more or less competitive, popular, and entertaining to fans at their home games and for television audiences. In addition, the chapter explains why most teams did not relocate during this period (Table 4.1).[1]

[1] For team relocations during the NBA's history, see Frank P. Jozsa Jr., *The National Basketball Association: Business, Organization and Strategy* (Singapore: World Scientific, 2011), 66–83; Frank P. Jozsa Jr. and John J. Guthrie Jr., *Relocating Teams and Expanding Leagues in Professional Sports: How the Major Leagues Respond to Market Conditions* (Westport, CT: Quorum Books, 1999); James Quirk and Rodney D. Fort, *Pay Dirt: The Business of Professional Team Sports* (Princeton, NJ: Princeton University Press, 1992); Kenneth L. Shropshire, *The Sports Franchise Game: Cities in Pursuit of Sports Franchises, Events, Stadiums, and Arenas* (Philadelphia, PA: University of Pennsylvania Press, 1995). See such websites as sportsecyclopedia.com, nba.com, basketball-reference.com, landofbasketball.com, bleacherreport.com, and cbssports.com for more details about teams and their arenas, seasons, performances, coaches, and players.

F.P. Jozsa Jr., *National Basketball Association Strategies*,
SpringerBriefs in Economics 84, DOI 10.1007/978-3-319-10058-6_4

Table 4.1 NBA Team relocations before 1976, characteristics, selected years/seasons

	Team relocations		Seasons		
Year	Before	After	Before	After	Postmove history
1951	Tri-Cities Blackhawks	Milwaukee Hawks	2	4	Moved to St. Louis in 1955
1955	Milwaukee Hawks	St. Louis Hawks	4	13	Moved to Atlanta in 1968
1957	Fort Wayne Pistons	Detroit Pistons	8	57	Current NBA team
1957	Rochester Royals	Cincinnati Royals	8	15	Moved to KC in 1972
1960	Minneapolis Lakers	Los Angeles Lakers	11	54	Current NBA team
1962	Philadelphia Warriors	SF Warriors	13	9	Moved to Oakland in 1971
1963	Chicago Zephyrs	Baltimore Bullets	2	10	Moved to Wash. in 1973
1963	Syracuse Nationals	Philadelphia 76ers	14	51	Current NBA team
1968	St. Louis Hawks	Atlanta Hawks	13	46	Current NBA team
1971	San Diego Rockets	Houston Rockets	4	43	Current NBA team
1971	SF Warriors	Golden State Warriors	9	43	Current NBA team
1972	Cincinnati Royals	KC-Omaha Kings	15	13	Moved to Sacramento in 1984
1973	Baltimore Bullets	Cap./Wash. Bull./Wiz.	10	41	Current NBA team

Note: NBA is National Basketball Association. Year is when teams relocated and their first regular season at the postmove site. Seasons are the number of NBA regular seasons at the premove and postmove sites. SF is San Francisco. KC is Kansas City. After relocating from Baltimore to Washington, DC in 1973, the team changed its name to Capital (Cap.) Bullets and then to Washington (Wash.) Bullets in 1974, and to Washington Wizards (Wiz.) in 1997

Source: Frank P. Jozsa Jr., *The National Basketball Association* (Singapore: World Scientific, 2011), and James Quirk and Rodney D. Fort, *Pay Dirt* (Princeton, NJ: Princeton University Press, 1992)

Team Relocations

Tri-Cities Blackhawks → Milwaukee Hawks

Owned by a partnership, the Blackhawks joined the NBA in 1949 after playing three seasons in the NBL. One year after the club qualified for the playoffs, Ben Kerner became its majority owner. In that NBA season, the Blackhawks played poorly and were unable to attract many fans to their home games in Moline and Rock Island, Illinois and Davenport, Iowa. Thus, the team's financial losses caused Kerner to move the Blackhawks in 1951 to southeast Wisconsin where he renamed his club the Milwaukee Hawks. Playing its games in a much larger city than the previous 2 years, Kerner expected more attendances and more gate receipts and revenue. In other words, the Tri-Cities were simply too small in population and as sports markets from the late 1940s to early 1950s to financially support an NBA team at least three seasons.

Milwaukee Hawks → St. Louis Hawks

Despite drafting future superstar Bob Petit, the Milwaukee Hawks won less than 35 % of their games in the league's 1951–1953 regular seasons and thus they failed to become champions. By 1954, local sports fans were apparently more interested in the newly arrived Milwaukee Braves baseball team. The Hawks, therefore, were not popular or entertaining for people in the city while finishing near the bottom of or last in their division.

In addition, Hawks owner Ben Kerner realized that local sports fans would not support a professional basketball team that won just one of three regular season games and was not competitive, exciting, or valuable. As the Hawks' operating income and revenue continued to deteriorate and remain among the lowest in the league, Kerner decided to move his franchise from Milwaukee to eastern Missouri in 1955 and rename it the St. Louis Hawks. In short, Hawks' games did not interest people in Milwaukee and therefore the club existed in a market where professional baseball and not basketball had more opportunities to attract fans, win championships, and become financially prosperous for years.

Fort Wayne Pistons → Detroit Pistons

After transferring from the NBL to BAA in 1948 and then 1 year later into the NBA, the Pistons played their home games for eight basketball seasons in Fort Wayne, which was a relatively small town in northeast Indiana. While operating there, the club was popular when it won Western Division (WD) titles in 1955 and 1956. In addition, the club's annual attendance averaged about 118,000 at Allen County's War Memorial Coliseum because of great performances by all-star forward George Yardley and such other players as Frankie Brian and Andy Phillip.

Even so, the team did not earn enough revenue for franchise owner Fred Zollner to earn a profit. Besides occasional attendance problems at their home games, some Pistons players had allegedly conspired with gamblers to lose games in the NBA's 1954 and 1955 regular seasons. Supposedly, these players caused the club to lose a final series to the Syracuse Nationals in the 1954–1955 NBA championship. These troubles, in part, were reasons for Zollner to move his club in 1957 from Fort Wayne to nearby Detroit, Michigan and rename it the Detroit Pistons.

At Olympia Stadium, Cobo Arena, and then the Pontiac Superdome, the Pistons struggled to win games from the late 1950s to mid-1980s. The team gradually improved, however, after owner William Davidson hired head coach Chuck Daly and such players as Bill Laimbeer, Joe Dumars, Isiah Thomas, Vinnie Johnson, and Dennis Rodman.

Playing its home games at The Palace of Auburn Hills between 1988 and 2008, the team made 17 playoff appearances and won nine division and five conference titles and three NBA championships. Thus, the franchise was increasingly popular and its revenue and estimated market value were higher than most NBA teams. When Davidson died in 2009, his daughter Karen became the Pistons' majority owner.

Regarding operating problems, there have been dark days at The Palace of Auburn Hills since the Pistons played in six straight Eastern Conference (EC) finals from 2003 to 2008. Before firing head coach Maurice Cheeks, the team lost 64 % of its games during four recent seasons causing its ticket base to decrease by one-half. Multimillionaire owner Tom Gores has invested $40 million into renovating the team's arena since he bought the franchise in 2011. As a result, season ticket sales surged by more than 35 % according to Palace Sports & Entertainment Chief Executive Officer/President Dennis Mannion. However, the sale of suites on the arena's top level continue to lag with only 10 of 64 leased in the 2012–2013 NBA season.[2]

Rochester Royals → Cincinnati Royals

After winning an NBL championship in 1946 and a division title in 1947 and again as a BAA team in 1948, 1 year later the Royals shifted from the BAA to NBA. In 1949, the team won its division and a league championship in 1951. After their early success in the league, the Royals performed poorly for five consecutive seasons winning about 45 % of their games and having a decline in attendances at the 13,000-seat Rochester War Memorial. While there, the club was unable to earn a profit for owners Jack and Lester Harrison.

Because of these and other problems, the Harrison's moved their team in 1957 from small-market Rochester in western New York to more populated Cincinnati in southwestern Ohio. Cincinnati had a large college basketball fan base that rooted for the hometown Bearcats and furthermore was home of the Major League Baseball (MLB) Reds. Despite low attendances at the 10,800-seat Cincinnati Gardens, the Royals made seven playoff appearances and competed in two conference finals primarily because of Hall of Fame players Oscar Robertson, Jerry Lucas, and Jack Twyman. Moreover, the franchise sold three times from 1958 to 1969.

Minneapolis Lakers → Los Angeles Lakers

While playing in the NBL, the Lakers won a championship in 1948 and 1 year later, joined the NBA. From 1949 to 1960, the club was very successful because it appeared in 11 playoffs and won four division titles and five league championships. For the most part, these victories occurred because of head coach John Kundla and superstars George Mikan, Clyde Lovellette, Elgin Baylor, Slater Martin, Vern Mikkelsen, and Jim Pollard.

---

[2] Recent financial data about the Detroit Pistons, Los Angeles Lakers, Philadelphia 76ers, Atlanta Hawks, Houston Rockets, Golden State Warriors, Washington Wizards, and other NBA franchises was in Kurt Badenhausen, Mike Ozanian, and Christina Settimi, "NBA Team Values: The Business of Basketball" at http://www.forbes.com cited 6 February 2014.

There were financial troubles, however, with the franchise's business during the 1950s. In 1957, for example, several Minneapolis companies and individuals from Minnesota contributed $200,000 to a fund for the team to continue operating in the NBA. Owners Ben Berger and Morris Chalfen, who fully purchased the club in 1956, sold it to a group headed by entrepreneur Bob Short.

Two years after the NBA put the team on financial probation and fearing bankruptcy, Short moved his franchise from Minneapolis to highly populated southern California. He changed the team's name to Los Angeles Lakers who, in turn, played their home games in the city's 16,021-seat Sports Arena, then in the 17,505-seat Forum, and later in the 19,079-seat Staples Center.

From 1960 to 2013, Lakers' teams made 43 playoff appearances and won 28 division and 25 conference titles, and 11 league championships. Besides establishing several records because of outstanding performances by its superstar players and great coaches, the franchise ranked second in the NBA with a market value of $1.35 billion in 2013. In retrospect, the relocation of this franchise from Minneapolis to Los Angeles in 1960 was a brilliant strategy that benefited the league and Lakers' owners, executives, coaches, and players, and provided entertainment to basketball fans in Los Angeles and across the country.

The team's $110 million payroll in its 2012–2013 season triggered the NBA's biggest luxury tax equaling $29.3 million. Nevertheless, the payroll was not enough to keep the Lakers from being defeated in the first round of the playoffs after 15-time all-star Kobe Bryant tore his Achilles tendon at the end of the regular season.

For additional revenue, the Lakers recently initiated a blockbuster $3.6 billion, 20-year television deal with Time Warner. While ratings on Time Warner Cable SportsNet were the fourth highest in the league, they also represented the biggest audience at an average of 261,000 per game. Indeed, this will continue to be a popular, prosperous, and successful franchise especially for owner Jerry Buss and his team's coaching staff and players.

Philadelphia Warriors → San Francisco Warriors

Founded in 1946, the Philadelphia Warriors played in the BAA for three seasons and won a championship in 1947. After transferring from the BAA into the NBA in 1949, the club played competitively and won two division titles and then in 1956, a league championships. The Warriors' best players were Paul Arizin and Neil Johnston, and later the great scorer and rebounder Wilt Chamberlain.

Besides its NBA titles and a championship between 1949 and 1962, the Warriors franchise was not a successful business investment for its owners while based in Philadelphia. Although average attendance at home games exceeded 190,000 per season, the team was not as popular as the MLB Phillies, National Football League (NFL) Eagles, or National Hockey League (NHL) Flyers. This, in turn, negatively influenced the Warriors' cash flow, revenue, and profit.

As a result, a syndicate headed by business executive Franklin Mieuli acquired the team in 1962 from Eddie Gottlieb for $850,000. Dissatisfied playing home games in the city's outdated Arena and Convention Center, Mieuli's group moved the team that year from Philadelphia to the California Bay Area and renamed it San Francisco Warriors.

In short, the Philadelphia area had too many popular and traditional professional sports teams during the early 1960s for the Warriors to compete for local sports fans and thus win market share from the city's Phillies, Eagles, and Flyers. Indeed, the Warriors' best opportunity to earn more revenue from gate receipts, merchandize sales, and other sources was to relocate to America's west coast and play home games in Daly City's 12,953-seat Cow Palace, which was near the border with San Francisco.

Chicago Zephyrs → Baltimore Bullets

An NBA expansion team in 1961, the Chicago Packers changed their nickname to Zephyrs for the league's 1962–1963 season. Although the club won more games and had higher attendances at its home games than the previous season, owner Dave Trager's franchise operated at a deficit and accumulated large debts for 2 years while based in Chicago. To avoid additional financial losses, Trager relocated his team in March 1963 from northeast Illinois to eastern Maryland. He renamed it Baltimore Bullets, in part, because of the area's ammunition factories, which produced military bullets for weapons in World War II.

In 1949, a BAA expansion team named Baltimore Bullets joined the NBA. Five years later, this franchise folded midway through the league's 1954–1955 regular season. Interestingly, there was no relationship because the two professional basketball teams each nicknamed the Bullets. Meanwhile, Trager's club played at the city's 14,000-seat Civic Center until it moved from Baltimore to Washington, DC, in 1973.

Syracuse Nationals → Philadelphia 76ers

After playing three seasons in the NBL, the Syracuse Nationals joined the NBA in 1949. During the 1950s to early 1960s, the team made 14 playoff appearances and won three division titles and a league championship in 1955. Besides owner Danny Biasone and Coach Alex Hannum, its Hall of Fame players include Hal Greer, Adolph Shayes, Al Cervi, and Early Lloyd.

While winning 53 % of its games in the 1960–1962 NBA seasons, the Nationals' average attendance at the Onondaga War Memorial was only 128,000 spectators. As players aged and the team won its last division title and championship in 1955, midsized Syracuse was simply too small of a sports market to continue supporting the Nationals and allow the franchise to make a profit.

In 1963, a syndicate led by paper magnate Irv Kosloff purchased the team for $500,000 from Jack Egan and moved it from upstate New York to southeast Pennsylvania. Kosloff nicknamed his team 76ers because in 1776, government officials signed the Declaration of Independence in Philadelphia. Consequently, the Syracuse Nationals were the final NBL team to relocate and the last small-town team in the NBA.

Since relocating from Syracuse, the 76ers have appeared in 33 playoffs and won eight division and six conference titles, and NBA championships in 1967 and 1983. After experiencing problems with motivating some of its coaches and players, the team has not won its division since 2001. After head coach Larry Brown left in 2003, the club struggled to win games with eight different coaches who, as a group, were unable to inspire their players against such division rivals as the Boston Celtics, New York Knicks, and Toronto Raptors.

In 2013, owners Joshua Harris and David Blitzer expanded their sports empire by purchasing the NHL New Jersey Devils and the team's home arena, the Prudential Center for $320 million. Although the 76ers are primarily a tenant at the 20,328-seat Wells Fargo Center, the franchise cannot move to New Jersey or elsewhere because its current lease commits the team to Philadelphia until 2029.

Before the 2012–2013 NBA season, the 76ers hired more than 40 sales and marketing people to boost ticket sales and corporate partnerships. In addition, the team downsized its roster before the league's 2013–2014 season and consequently, had a relatively low payroll. Given these and other strategies, it is unlikely the 76ers will win another division title for several years unless head coach Brett Brown provides leadership and his players respond by playing much better as a team.

St. Louis Hawks → Atlanta Hawks

After moving from Milwaukee to St. Louis, Missouri in 1955, the Hawks excelled as a team in its division. From the mid-1950s to late 1960s, the club was in 12 playoffs and won six division and four WC titles, and an NBA championship in 1958. Led by head coaches Alex Hannum and Red Holzman, the team succeeded because of such Hall of Fame players as Cliff Hagan, Bob Petit, Richie Guerin, and Lenny Wilkins.

To replace aging Kiel Auditorium and the huge but outdated St. Louis Arena, owner Ben Kerner negotiated with city officials during the mid-1960s but failed to get their commitment to finance the construction of a modern basketball facility in the area. Because of that decision, Kerner sold his franchise in 1968 for $3.5 million to a syndicate headed by wealthy Atlanta real estate developer Tom Cousins. Soon after this deal, Cousins moved the team from eastern Missouri to north-central Georgia and changed its name to Atlanta Hawks.

Since 1968, the Hawks have played their home games in five different venues including the current 18,818-seat Phillips Arena. While these buildings attracted fans and generated revenue for the franchise, the Hawks appeared in 28 playoffs and won four division titles. Such people as owner Ted Turner, forward Dominique

Wilkins, center Walt Bellamy, guard Pete Maravich, and coaches Lenny Wilkins and Hubie Brown are former Hawks in the Hall of Fame.

For its business prospects, the Hawks organization built seven all-inclusive loge boxes with 28 seats each at Phillips Arena 20 rows from the court prior to the 2013–2014 NBA season. Priced in the low six figures, the loge boxes include food, beer, and wine to all events at the facility. To provide space for the new boxes the team, which operates the city-owned arena, removed 140 club seats. The net revenue added by the new boxes expects to generate annually about $1 million. While the Hawks were in the playoffs six times during the 2000s, they have not made the conference finals since 1970 when the NBA operated with only 14 teams. Although profitable, the team needs to be more consistent to win an EC title and play in its first NBA Finals.

San Diego Rockets → Houston Rockets

After losing 67 games during its first regular season in the NBA, the San Diego Rockets won 45 of their games and qualified for the playoffs in 1969 but then defeated in the WD semifinals by the Atlanta Hawks. The team's best players were center Elvin Hayes, guard Pat Riley, and in its 1970–1971 season, guard Calvin Murphy.

While playing home games at the city's 14,500-seat Sports Arena, the Rockets annual attendance was 233,000 per season. For sure, local sports fans were more enthusiastic about the American Football League (AFL)/NFL Chargers and MLB Padres than its NBA team. In addition, Rockets owner Robert Breitbard had financial losses operating his franchise in San Diego.

In 1971, Texas Sports Investment (TSI) purchased the Rockets from Breitbard for $5.6 million. Because of the team's dismal performances and attendance problems while in San Diego, real estate broker Wayne Duddleston and banker Billy Goldberg, both from southeastern Texas, headed TSI and decided to shift their team that year from southern California to Houston and rename it the Houston Rockets.

Between 1971 and 2014, the Rockets were in 26 playoffs, won four each division and conference titles, and consecutive NBA championships in their 1993–1994 seasons. Coaches Bill Fitch and Rudy Tomjanovich, and such Hall of Fame players as guard/forward Clyde Drexler and center Hakeem Olajuwon contributed many points to the team's victories during the 1980s and/or 1990s.

For recent news about the club's business, the Rockets' cable television ratings suffer because only 40 % of the Houston market receives CSN Houston. Indeed, carriers refuse to pay what they believe is an exorbitant subscriber fee for NBA games. The team, which owns 31 % of the regional sports network, had a 57 % drop in its average rating during the 2012–2013 NBA season, which was the first time Rockets' games were broadcast on CSN Houston. Besides television ratings, there are other problems with the franchise. Declaring fraud, Houston Astros owner Jim Crane has sued Comcast and Drayton McLane, from whom he bought the MLB team in 2011 along with 46 % of CSN Houston.

San Francisco Warriors → Golden State Warriors

While playing their home games for nine NBA seasons in San Francisco, the Warriors won conference titles in 1964 and 1967 but lost in the league's final series to, respectively, the Boston Celtics and Philadelphia 76ers. However, from 1962 to 1971, the team was not very popular among Bay Area sports fans and so it played some games at sites in Oakland and San Jose.

During the 1968–1970 NBA seasons, the club's annual attendances at home decreased to 192,000 while winning less than 50 % of its games. In addition, superstar Rick Barry left the Warriors in the late 1960s because of a dispute about incentive awards. Thus, due to low attendances at its home games and declining gate receipts and operating revenue, owner Franklin Mieuli moved his team in 1971 from San Francisco to Oakland and renamed it the Golden State Warriors.

After four seasons there, the team won the Pacific Division (PD), WC, and an NBA championship. Since winning another PD title in 1976, the Warriors have lost a majority of their games to such division rivals as the Los Angeles Clippers, Los Angeles Lakers, Phoenix Suns, and former Seattle Supersonics. In 2013, the Warriors made the conference playoffs but defeated in the second round by the San Antonio Spurs. That team included former Davidson College guard Stephen Curry, rebounder Andrew Bogut, and high scorer Klay Thompson. Because of Curry's leadership, better teamwork, and head coach Mark Jackson, the Warriors are more competitive now to challenge others for the PD and win another conference title.

During the summer of 2013, investor Vivek Ranadive sold his stake in the Warriors for a price that valued the franchise at $800 million. In fact, he sold his investment so that a group he headed could buy the NBA's Sacramento Kings for $534 million. Meanwhile, the Warriors are building a new $1 billion arena on the San Francisco waterfront that expects to open by 2017. Some recent but good news was the club's second highest home attendance in franchise history during its 2012–2013 season at 794,230.

Cincinnati Royals → Kansas City-Omaha Kings

From 1957 to 1972, the NBA Royals had financial problems. Indeed, the team had several different owners, operated in a small-to-midsized sports market of southwest Ohio, and consisted of a few very talented players but also mediocre coaches. During the late 1960s, the Royals played some of their home games at sites in Cleveland, Columbus, and Dayton, Ohio. This situation suggested the franchise was in trouble and not likely to survive much longer based in Cincinnati.

In the early 1970s, the team's average attendance fell to 145,000 per season and its winning percentage to 40 %. Furthermore, owner Max Jacobs had financial losses from operating his franchise and such Hall of Fame players as Oscar Robertson, Jack Twyman, Jerry Lucas, and Maurice Stokes were no longer with the club. Thus, the Royals had little opportunity to make the playoffs as it did six times during the 1960s.

Before the 1972 NBA season, Jacobs sold his franchise for $5 million to a syndicate named Missouri Valley Sports, Inc. That group included several wealthy investors who owned businesses and other properties in the Midwest. Shortly after receiving approval from the league, the syndicate moved its team from southwestern Ohio to Kansas City, Missouri and renamed it the Kansas City-Omaha Kings to avoid confusion with MLB's Royals.

The Kings initially divided their home games between Kansas City's 7,316-seat Municipal Auditorium and the 9,300-seat Omaha Civic Auditorium until they abandoned the Omaha market in 1975. The team's exit from Omaha marked the opening of the 16,785-seat Kemper Arena in Kansas City. During the early 1980s, the Kings played several home games before large crowds in St. Louis.

Kings teams achieved some success in their new home when they hired Cotton Fitzsimmons to coach. He won the NBA's Midwest Division in 1979 with such players as Rookie of the Year Phil Ford, shooting guard Otis Birdsong who was effective on offense and defense, forward Scott Wedman, and center Sam Lacey. That season, the team drew an average 10,789 fans to its home games in Kemper Arena. In fact, that was the only time during the club's tenure in Kansas City that its average attendance was in five figures.

The Kings made the playoffs in 1980 and again in 1981 despite finishing the regular season at 40–42. Furthermore, they made a surprise run in the NBA playoffs reaching the WC Finals. After upsetting the Portland Trailblazers and then Phoenix Suns in Arizona by winning the seventh game in the conference semifinals, the Kings lost to the Houston Rockets in five games.

A series of bad luck incidents, however, prevented the team from building on its success. First, Cleveland Cavaliers owner Ted Stepien lured star players' Wedman and Birdsong away from the Kings with big contract offers. Second, Kemper Arena's roof literally collapsed because of a severe storm with 70 mile-per-hour winds in downtown Kansas City, which forced the team to play most games in its 1979–1980 season at the much smaller Municipal Auditorium. Third, the Kings fired general manager Joe Axelson in a bizarre scandal because he reused marked postage stamps.

When the Kings rehired Joe Axelson as general manager, they brought back the executive who had previously traded superstars Oscar Robertson, Norm Van Lier, Nate Archibald, and Jerry Lucas. In addition, he became the first general manager in sports history to fail with the same franchise in four different cities and was not permanently let go until he rehired Coach Phil Johnson, whom he fired in midseason in Kansas City 10 years earlier.

Baltimore Bullets → Capital/Washington Bullets/Wizards

From 1963 to 1973, the Bullets played their home games in the city's 12,500-seat Civic Center. During the period, the team was in nine playoffs, won four division titles and in 1971, a conference championship. Although players like Earl Monroe,

Wes Unseld, Gus Johnson, and Kevin Porter were outstanding, the Bullets failed to become an NBA champion because of such other competitors as the Los Angeles Lakers, Milwaukee Bucks, and New York Knicks.

An important reason for the Bullets' success was owner Dave Trager's sale of the franchise in 1964 for \$1.1 million to a syndicate headed by executive Abe Pollin. Besides applying his business experience and knowledge of sports operations to owning and operating the Bullets, he invested additional resources and money to improve the team. Pollin, for example, hired efficient staff and productive coaches, increased players' payroll, and traded low-performing centers, forwards, and guards for those who would contribute more to the Bullets' performances on defense and offense.

Although the Bullets' average attendances in the league's 1970–1972 regular seasons were between 250,000 and 275,000 at the Civic Center in Baltimore and despite winning at least 50 % of their total games, the franchise needed more revenue to compete with division rivals in the EC. Consequently, Pollin moved his club from Baltimore to Landover, Maryland in 1973 and renamed it the Capital Bullets.

Nicknamed the Wizards and not Bullets in 1997, the team made 18 playoff appearances, won three each division and conference titles, and an NBA championship between 1974 and 2008. Dick Motta coached the 1978 championship team and his best players included hall of famers Elvin Hayes and Wes Unseld. Since winning their division and conference in 1979, most Bullets/Wizards teams struggled to compete against such rivals as the Atlanta Hawks, Cleveland Cavaliers, Miami Heat, and Orlando Magic.

Venture capital investor, philanthropist, former senior executive of American Online, and founder and Chief Executive Officer of Monumental Sports and Entertainment Ted Leonsis purchased the Wizards from Abe Pollin in 1999. Since then, the team has been in four playoffs and recorded more than 200 consecutive sellouts at the 18,506-seat Verizon Center in Washington, DC. In fact, the facility is a commercial success and regarded as one of the driving catalysts of the revitalization of the city's Chinatown neighborhood.

During 2013, owner Leonsis launched a digital sports and entertainment company named Monumental Network. It features programming related to Leonsis-owned assets like the Wizards, NHL Capitals, Women's NBA Mystics, and events at the Verizon Center. The company's goal is ultimately to grow into a cable network although Comcast controls the rights to Wizards' games through at least 2020. In the 2012–2013 NBA season, the network's average television ratings were disappointing for Wizard's games broadcast on CSN Mid-Atlantic. In fact, the ratings were second lowest in the league and only ahead of the Charlotte Bobcats.

Led by head coach Randy Wittman and superstar John Wall, the Wizards have potential but not enough talent on its current roster to consistently be in the playoffs and perhaps win a series of games. With more experience, however, Wizards captain Wall and such players as guards/forwards Martell Webster and Glen Rice are competitive enough to provide the team with leadership and better performances in future NBA seasons.

Table 4.2 contains financial information about seven NBA teams in this chapter. Grouped, their average estimated market value in 2013 was \$672 million, revenue

Table 4.2 Seven NBA teams, 2013 financial data

Team	Value (Rank)	Revenue	Operating income	Player expenses
Atlanta Hawks	425 (27)	119	–3.6	73
Detroit Pistons	450 (25)	139	10.3	76
Golden State Warriors	750 (9)	160	43.0	77
Houston Rockets	775 (6)	191	63.7	68
Los Angeles Lakers	1,350 (2)	295	66.4	110
Philadelphia 76ers	469 (23)	117	–3.8	83
Washington Wizards	485 (21)	122	7.0	72

Note: NBA is National Basketball Association. Amounts are in millions. Rank is among 30 NBA teams. Revenue and operating income are for the 2012–2013 season and net of revenue sharing and arena debt service. Value is an estimate based on teams' current arena deal (unless new arena is pending) without deduction for debt (other than arena debt). Revenue is net of arena revenues used for debt payments. Operating income is earnings before interest, taxes, depreciation, and amortization. Player expenses include benefits and bonuses

Source: "NBA Team Values: The Business of Basketball" at http://www.forbes.com cited 12 February 2014

$163 million, operating income $26 million, and player expenses $79 million. The Lakers had the highest amounts in each of the data while the lowest in value were the Hawks, in revenue and operating income the 76ers, and in player expenses the Wizards.

For how their amounts compared to those of other NBA teams in 2013, the New York Knicks ranked highest in value at $1.4 billion and Milwaukee Bucks lowest at $405 million; Knicks second at $287 million and Bucks lowest at $109 in revenue; Knicks highest at $96 million and Brooklyn Nets lowest at –$19 million in operating income; and the Miami Heat third at $90 million and Sacramento Kings thirtieth at $61 million in player expenses. Based on information in the table, the Lakers, Rockets, and Warriors had the most impressive data while the 76ers, Hawks, and Wizards were worst in the group from a financial perspective.

In the Appendix, Tables A4.1 and A4.2 contain specific details about the 13 NBA team relocations that occurred before 1976. To compare them before and after they moved, the first table has their number of seasons, playoffs, and championships. Then, the second provides their respective population and population rank during the year they shifted from one metropolitan area to another.

Among the group, 11 or 84 % of the teams played more seasons at their postmove than premove sites. The Warriors, however, existed fewer regular seasons in San Francisco than Philadelphia and so did the Kings in Kansas City-Omaha than when nicknamed the Royals in Cincinnati. Thus, the majority of these NBA teams became more popular, prosperous, and stable at their new sites. This, in turn, suggests moving their operations was the right decision for them based on differences in number of seasons prior and subsequent to switching locations especially for the Detroit Pistons, Los Angeles Lakers, and Philadelphia 76ers.

Relative to number of playoffs, the Milwaukee Hawks, San Francisco Warriors, and KC-Omaha Kings were in fewer of them than, respectively, the Tri-Cities

Blackhawks, Philadelphia Warriors, and Cincinnati Royals. Except for the Royals from 1957 to 1972, nine other teams qualified for more playoffs because, in part, they played more seasons at their postmove sites. Interestingly, the Baltimore Bullets played eight more seasons and appeared in eight additional playoffs than the Chicago Zephyrs. Consequently, the majority of teams improved their performances from pre- to postmove sites.

Nine or 69 % of the expansion teams won more NBA championships after they relocated. Four of them had zero before moving and thus later, became champions during one or more seasons. In contrast to them, the Cincinnati Royals, Atlanta Hawks, and Golden State Warriors were less productive by winning fewer titles than at their premove site. In other words, the Rochester Royals, St. Louis Hawks, and San Francisco Warriors were more successful in winning championships than in subsequent years playing home games in different cities and perhaps with new owners.

Based on the data in Table A4.1, the Pistons, Lakers, 76ers, and Rockets are current teams with more success than before at their premove sites in, respectively, Fort Wayne, Minneapolis, Syracuse, and San Diego. Besides these teams, their relocations benefited the league and other NBA franchises. In contrast to them, the worst moves were the Warriors from Philadelphia to San Francisco in 1962 and then 10 years later, the Royals from Cincinnati to become the Kings in Kansas City-Omaha.

According to Table A4.2, 7 or 53 % of the teams moved from less to more populated sports markets. Alternatively, five others relocated from bigger to smaller metropolitan areas and most likely, Milwaukee had a larger population and fan base than the Tri-Cities in the early 1950s. Before 1976, it was apparent that basketball fans in Cincinnati, St. Louis, Baltimore, San Diego, and the San Francisco-Oakland metropolitan areas were not as passionate about or willing to support their NBA team as those in MLB and the NFL. In short, a difference in population between markets was and continues to be a major factor for franchise owners when they decide to move from their home site and operate in another city to generate more gate receipts at games and additional revenues and profits.[3]

[3] Some additional information about these teams and their relocation is in "Basketball History" at http://www.history-of-basketball.com cited 20 September 2005; "History of Basketball" at http://library.thinkquest.org cited 24 August 2009; "National Basketball Association (NBA) History" at http://www.rauzulusstreet.com cited 12 August 2005; "NBA Growth Timetable" at http://www.basketball.com cited 17 September 2005; "Professional Basketball Leagues" at http://apbr.org cited 22 August 2009. For current literature, see the *Official NBA Guide*: *2013–14 Edition* (New York, NY: NBA Properties, 2013), and *Official NBA Register*: *2013–14 Edition* (New York, NY: NBA Properties, 2013).

Chapter 5
From 1976 Season

Between 1949 and 1975, 13 teams in the National Basketball Association (NBA) moved from their sites in metropolitan areas to other cities. While 6 or 46 % of them moved again, the other seven did not and continued to perform in the league's 2013–2014 season. These were the Detroit Pistons, Los Angeles Lakers, Philadelphia 76ers, Atlanta Hawks, Houston Rockets, Golden State Warriors, and Capital Bullets who were renamed Washington Bullets in 1973 and then 24 years later, the Washington Wizards.

After its 1975–1976 season, the NBA increased in size from 18 to 22 franchises when four teams from the former American Basketball Association (ABA) joined a division. With 11 clubs each in the NBA's Eastern Conference (EC) and Western Conference (WC), the New York Nets joined the Atlantic Division (AD), San Antonio Spurs the Central Division (CD), and Denver Nuggets and Indiana Pacers the Midwest Division (MWD). Meanwhile, the Pacific Division (PD) consisted of five teams before and after the leagues merged in 1976.

To reveal how they changed as competitors and sports enterprises geographically and from a business perspective during 1976–2013, this chapter analyzes when, where, and why eight NBA teams moved from their sites in various cities of metropolitan areas to others and existed there or relocated again. As such, the contents identify each of these organizations and provide reasons they moved and became more or less competitive, popular, and entertaining to fans at their home games and for television audiences. In addition, the chapter explains why most teams did not relocate during this period (Table 5.1).[1]

[1] For team relocations during the NBA's history, there is information in Frank P. Jozsa Jr., *The National Basketball Association: Business, Organization and Strategy* (Singapore: World Scientific, 2011), 84–93; Frank P. Jozsa Jr. and John J. Guthrie Jr., *Relocating Teams and Expanding Leagues in Professional Sports: How the Major Leagues Respond to Market Conditions* (Westport, CT: Quorum Books, 1999); James Quirk and Rodney D. Fort, *Pay Dirt: The Business of Professional Team Sports* (Princeton, NJ: Princeton University Press, 1992); Kenneth L. Shropshire, *The Sports Franchise Game: Cities in Pursuit of Sports Franchises, Events, Stadiums, and Arenas* (Philadelphia, PA: University of Pennsylvania Press,

F.P. Jozsa Jr., *National Basketball Association Strategies*,
SpringerBriefs in Economics 84, DOI 10.1007/978-3-319-10058-6_5

Table 5.1 NBA team relocations from 1976, characteristics, selected years/season

Team relocations			Seasons		
Year	Before	After	Before	After	Post-move history
1977	New York Nets	New Jersey Nets	1	35	Moved to Brooklyn in 2012
1978	Buffalo Braves	San Diego Clippers	8	6	Moved to LA in 1984
1979	New Orleans Jazz	Utah Jazz	5	35	Current NBA team
1984	San Diego Clippers	Los Angeles Clippers	6	30	Current NBA team
1985	Kansas City Kings	Sacramento Kings	13	29	Current NBA team
2001	Vancouver Grizzlies	Memphis Grizzlies	6	13	Current NBA team
2002	Charlotte Hornets	NO Hornets/Pelicans	15	12	Current NBA team
2008	Seattle Supersonics	Oklahoma City Thunder	41	6	Current NBA team
2012	New Jersey Nets	Brooklyn Nets	35	2	Current NBA team

Note: NBA is National Basketball Association. The slash (/) indicates change in nickname. Year is when teams relocated and their first regular season at the postmove site. Seasons are the number of NBA regular seasons at the premove and postmove sites. LA is Los Angeles. NO is New Orleans. After relocating from Charlotte to New Orleans in 2002, the team changed its nickname from Hornets to Pelicans in 2013. Although they played their home games within the same metropolitan area, the Nets in 1977 and 2012 were relocations because they had different sites before and after with respect to their potential revenue, fan support, and market

Source: Frank P. Jozsa Jr., *The National Basketball Association*: *Business*, *Organization and Strategy* (Singapore: World Scientific, 2011), and James Quirk and Rodney D. Fort, *Pay Dirt*: *The Business of Professional Team Sports* (Princeton, NJ: Princeton University Press, 1992)

Team Relocations

New York Nets → New Jersey Nets

After competing in the ABA for 1 year as the New Jersey Americans and another eight as the New York Nets, owner Roy Boe entered his club into the NBA when the leagues merged in 1976. That year, superstar Julius Erving refused to play for the Nets after Boe refused to increase his salary. Traded from the Nets to the Philadelphia 76ers for $3 million, Erving became a greater player while the Nets finished the season with a 22–60 record. In addition, the Nets' regular season attendances declined on average from 406,000 in the ABA to 284,000 in the NBA and this, of course, caused financial problems for the franchise.

Before the NBA's 1977–1978, season, Boe transferred his team from New York to its original State and renamed it the New Jersey Nets. Playing at home in Piscataway's 8,500-seat Rutgers Athletic Center, the team lost the majority of its games forcing Boe to declare bankruptcy in 1978. As a result, he sold his franchise for an unknown price to business executives Joseph Taub and Alan Cohen.

While playing their home games in the $85 million Brendan Arena–renamed Continental Airlines Arena in 1996 and then Izod Center in 2007–from the late

1995). In addition, examine such websites as sportsecyclopedia.com, nba.com, basketball-reference.com, landofbasketball.com, bleacherreport.com, and cbssports.com for facts and other data about NBA teams and their arenas, seasons, performances, coaches, and players.

1970s to early 2000s, the Nets were in 16 playoffs and won four division and two conference titles. During this period, such coaches as Kevin Loughery, Dave Wohl, Bill Fitch, and Lawrence Frank were leaders of Nets teams. Some of their players included all-stars Bernard King, Derrick Coleman, Kenny Anderson, and Jason Kidd.

From a business perspective, the New Jersey Nets franchise was located in a major sports market within a highly populated area. Thus, despite its inability to win a league championship, the club earned enough revenue from gate receipts, television broadcasts, and other sources to survive for 35 NBA seasons and marginally increase in value as an operating enterprise. Unfortunately, the Boston Celtics, New York Knicks, and other competitive teams also existed in the AD. In part, they prevented the Nets from winning more division and conference titles. Historically, Nets teams had below average-to-average performances in several of their seasons while the franchise experienced some financial and ownership problems during various years.

Buffalo Braves → San Diego Clippers

During the 1970–1977 NBA seasons, the Buffalo Braves had a series of different owners, were in three playoffs, and ranked among the lowest of teams in attendances at their home games in the 15,000-seat Buffalo Memorial Auditorium and 15,728-seat Maple Leaf Gardens. Because of these and other problems, franchise owner Paul Snyder tried to sell the club for $6.1 million in 1976 to investor Irving Cowen who planned to move it from Buffalo to Hollywood, Florida. That deal, however, failed when the City of Buffalo filed a $10 million damage suit in court and obtained an injunction to block Snyder's proposed sale of the Braves.

One year after purchasing the franchise from Snyder, former politician, entrepreneur, and businessperson John Y. Brown met with California film producer Irv Levin and executive Harold Lipton, who jointly owned the Celtics, and negotiated a transaction in which the coowners would swap franchises with Brown taking control of the Celtics while Levin and Lipton got the Braves. In 1978, the NBA approved the deal and then a relocation of the Braves from Buffalo to southern California where it became the San Diego Clippers.

From 1978 to 1985, the Clippers played their home games in the city's 14,500-seat Sports Arena. Despite such coaches as Gene Shue, Paul Silas, and Jim Lyman, and competitive players as Bill Walton, Tom Chambers, and World B. Free, the team failed to lead its division or win enough games to qualify for the NBA playoffs. After the Clippers finished with a 43–39 record in their first season, it was the last winning season for the franchise in 13 years. Although Free scored more than 30 points-per-game during one season, San Diego native Walton missed many games due to foot injuries.

In 1981, Irv Levin sold his team for $13.5 million to southern California real estate developer and attorney Donald Sterling. After the Clippers played poorly during their final years in San Diego while averaging only 4,500 fans at their home games, Sterling lobbied the league to relocate the team to his native Los Angeles and thus invade the NBA Lakers' territory.

New Orleans Jazz → Utah Jazz

As an NBA expansion team in 1974, the New Orleans Jazz played its home games one season in the 6,500-seat Loyola Field House and later in the city's 7,853-seat Municipal Auditorium and then in the 55,675-seat Louisiana Superdome. From the 1974 to 1978 NBA seasons, the club won only 40 % of its games but averaged 445,000 in annual attendances. The club was popular among local sports fans because of superstar Pete Maravich. Besides being a prolific scorer, Maravich was clever while dribbling a basketball and passing it to his teammates.

When Maravich was unable to play because of frequent injuries, causing the team's attendances at home games to decline, Jazz owner Sam Battisone decided not to renew his unprofitable lease at the Superdome and move his franchise in 1979 from New Orleans to Salt Lake City, Utah. Subsequently, it became the Utah Jazz.

Since the 1979–1980 NBA season, the Utah Jazz were in 25 playoffs and won eight division and two conference titles. Finishing runner-up in the 1997 and 1998 championship series to Michael Jordan's Chicago Bulls, the Jazz's key players were Most Valuable Player (MVP) Karl Malone and all-time assists leader John Stockton. The team's most knowledgeable, prominent, and successful coach was Jerry Sloan and then Frank Layden.

Because Salt Lake City does not host a MLB, NFL, or NHL team, Jazz games are a popular attraction in the area and profitable business events. Thus, the franchise will continue to operate there and extend its fan base while generating more revenue from gate receipts, corporate sponsors, and local and regional television markets.

Even though the Jazz are consistently one of the NBA's most supported teams, its attendances at home games and television ratings have declined in recent years. In fact, attendance was off 3 % during a recent regular season while the club's ratings on Roots Sports were down 21 % although fifth highest in the league.

To enhance fans' experiences at 19,911-seat Energy Solutions Arena, the Utah Jazz spent $15 million to renovate its 23-year-old arena. Renovations included upgraded audio and video systems and new kitchens on the suite level. Recently, the Jazz slashed payroll to among the lowest in the NBA in order to rebuild its roster and potentially set itself up to choose a player near the top of the 2014 NBA draft.

San Diego Clippers → Los Angeles Clippers

Named in reference to the city's history as a harbor for Clipper ships including the 1,197-ton Star of India, the San Diego Clippers won only 29 % of their games while attendances at the city's 14,500-seat Sports Arena averaged 4,600 fans per game. After finishing with 49 victories in the NBA's 1979–1980 season, Clippers teams did not have another winning season for 13 years.

Because of the club's poor performances, relatively small attendances at its home games, and financial problems, owner Donald Sterling lobbied league officials for permission to relocate the Clippers from San Diego to a more populated area on the west coast. Sterling's strategy succeeded in 1984 when the team moved to south-central California and became the Los Angeles Clippers.

For invading territory of the Los Angeles Lakers, the Clippers franchise had to pay $6 million to the NBA. The team, meanwhile, played its home games for several seasons in Los Angeles' 16,161-seat Memorial Sports Arena and since 1999, in Los Angeles' 18,977-seat Staples Arena.

From 1992 to 2013, the Clippers appeared in six playoffs and won one division title but zero conference and league championships. However, the club's fortunes turned in the early 2010s with the acquisition of such core players as power forward Blake Griffin and point guard Chris Paul. In the 2012–2013 NBA season, for example, the franchise won its division and made the playoffs for the ninth time in franchise history and the third time in the past eight seasons. The Clippers also elevated their emerging rivalry with the Lakers after finishing with a better record than they did for the fifth time and won their regular season series for the second time since moving to Los Angeles in 1984.

Regarding their business prospects, the Clippers' popularity has surged in recent years especially because of all-stars Griffin and Paul. In fact, the team's television ratings on Prime Ticket surged 55 % in its 2012–2013 season and were the fifth biggest audiences in the NBA. Meanwhile, the Clippers share the Staples Center with the NBA Lakers and NHL Kings in the only tri-tenant professional sports arrangement of its kind in North America.

In 2013, the franchise signed a 10-year extension of their lease at the Staples Center, which commits the team to play home games in the arena at least through the 2023–2024 NBA season. In short, if they continue to win regular season games and another division title, the Clippers' revenue and operating income will increase and make the team more valuable from a financial perspective.[2]

---

[2]Two months after the NBA banned him from the sport, Clippers' co-owner Don Sterling hired four private investigation firms to look for dirt on the league's other 29 owners and on Commissioner Adam Silver and former commissioner David Stern. Investigators, according to the Associated Press report, have a six-figure budget and a 30-day timeframe in which to examine the league's finances, allegations of previous discriminatory conduct, and compensation to Stern and Silver. Specifically, investigators will be looking for comments by other owners that are off-color, racist, homophobic, or sexist. Meanwhile, his $1 billion lawsuit, in which he contends the league violated his constitutional rights because he may have been illegally recorded making racist comments, and violated antitrust laws by trying to force him to sell the team, proceeds. He is essentially suing himself because his wife, Shelly, has negotiated a sale of the team to Steve Ballmer for about $2 billion and agreed to indemnify the league in any lawsuit. In August 2014, Ballmer became owner of the franchise. For the history and business consequences of Donald Sterling's remarks, see various articles in the *Charlotte Observer*, *New York Times*, and *Wall Street Journal*.

Kansas City Kings → Sacramento Kings

After moving from southwest Ohio to northwest Missouri in 1972, the Kansas City-Omaha Kings, renamed Kings 3 years later, were good enough to compete in five playoffs and win a division title in 1979. Besides these performances, however, the franchise experienced problems including a collapsed roof at the city's Kemper Arena, a scandal involving the team's general manager, and the sale of the Kings in 1982 from the Missouri Valley Sports Inc. to a syndicate led by wealthy California property developer Greg Lukenbill.

In the 1982–1984 NBA seasons, the Kings underperformed by winning only 46 % of their games and averaging 8,000 in attendances at the 16,785-seat Kemper Arena. This motivated Lukenbill and his investment group to petition the NBA for authorization to transfer the Kings to another metropolitan area. After the league's 1984–1985 season and its approval, the Kings moved from Kansas City to northern California where they became the Sacramento Kings.

From 1986 to 2006, the Sacramento Kings were in 10 playoffs including consecutive appearance in 2000–2006 and won division titles in 2002 and 2003. During this period, Rick Adelman was the team's head coach while all-star forward Chris Webber, a former All-American from the University of Michigan and member of the "Fab Five" led the Kings in scoring and rebounding. Besides Webber, other players who contributed points were Mike Bibby, Bobby Jackson, and foreigners Vlade Divac and Peja Stojakovic.

For the Kings to win a conference title and ultimately an NBA championship, the club's players must excel in teamwork to defeat such opponents as the Los Angeles Clippers, Golden State Warriors, and Phoenix Suns in regular season games. In addition, the Kings' owners must increase players' payroll above $70 million to attract outstanding free agents and talented veterans with experience. Otherwise, the team will struggle as a competitor and business in the sport.

During May 2013, an investment group led by technology entrepreneur Vivek Ranadive paid an inflated enterprise value of $534 million for 65 % of the Kings and 26-year-old, 17,317-seat Sleep Train Arena, which is the name of a chain of mattress and bed retailers in Rocklin, California. The following month, Ranadive purchased co-owner Bob Cook's 7 % stake in the franchise for $15.1 million.

Because of a significant long-term financial decision, the Kings received approval from the city council to build a $450 million arena in downtown Sacramento by 2016 including an investment of $250 million of public funds. Nevertheless, a petition drive backed by two antisubsidy groups gathered more than 35,000 signatures by the end of 2013. If 63 % or more of those signatures were from registered city voters, a measure would likely appear on the June 2014 ballot for voter approval of the subsidy.[3]

---

[3]During 2013, there were actions by politicians and other groups to move the Kings from Sacramento to Seattle. These were discussed in such articles as Chris Ballard, "The NBA's Trail of Cheers," *Sports Illustrated* (4 March 2013), 56; Lee Jenkins, Richard O'Brien, Mark Bechtel, and

Vancouver Grizzlies → Memphis Grizzlies

During the 1995–1996 to 2000–2001 NBA seasons, the expansion Grizzlies struggled to win games and failed to become a popular sports franchise in the Vancouver area of British Columbia. While sharing 18,630-seat General Motors Place with the NHL Canucks, the Grizzlies' average attendance was 12,000 at their home games. In addition, some players violated team standards by behaving irresponsibly and the league's lockout caused financial losses for the franchise.

Within 2 years after majority owner Jeff LaQueef sold his stake in the Grizzlies to Orca Bay Sports and Entertainment, multimillionaire Michael Heisley purchased and promised to keep the team in Vancouver. Nevertheless, when its attendances did not improve in the 2000–2001 season, Heisley received approval from the league, and thus moved his club from Vancouver to southeast Tennessee renaming it the Memphis Grizzlies.[4]

From 2004 to 2014, the Grizzlies were in seven playoffs including a conference final in 2013. Of the team's nine head coaches since 2001, less than two-thirds of them coached for two seasons and the others one season. While playing their home games at the city's $250 million, 18,119-seat FedEx Forum, the Grizzles have improved their performances since 2010 because of such talented and experienced players as center Marc Gasol, forward Zack Randolph, and guard Mike Conley.

To win more regular season games against such competitive division rivals as the Dallas Mavericks, Houston Rockets, and San Antonio Spurs, the franchise must increase the team's payroll account and sign free agents and veterans who are able to score points and play defense to assist Gasol, Randolph, and Conley.

To recap, the Grizzlies' 2012–2013 season was the most successful year in franchise history with a record 56 regular season wins and their first appearance in the WC Finals. The team's success boosted attendance 6 % and the extra playoff games stemmed annual losses that topped $20 million in recent seasons. New owner Robert Pera–a Ubiquiti Networks director who acquired the franchise in 2012 from Heisley for $350 million–reorganized the team's financial situation through a series of trades that pushed the Grizzlies under the league's luxury tax threshold although it was $4 million over before the January 2013 trades. The biggest change was trading swingman Rudy Gay and transferring his 5-year, $82 million maximum contract to the Toronto Raptors.

Mark Beech, "The Only Game in Town," *Sports Illustrated* (6 May 2013), 15; Ken Belson, "Two Groups Present Pitches For Kings," *New York Times* (4 April 2013), B15.

[4] See, for example, Howard Tsumura, "Vancouver," *Sporting News* (30 April 2001), 52; Harvey Araton, "Grizzlies' Relocation Reveals the N.B.A's Fault Lines," *New York Times* (25 March 2001), 11; and Ian Thomsen, "New Home Won't End Woes," *Sports Illustrated* (6 February 2006), 109.

Charlotte Hornets → New Orleans Hornets/Pelicans

An NBA expansion franchise in 1988, the Hornets had the league's highest attendances for several years while playing home games at the 24,042-seat Charlotte Coliseum. From 1993 to 2002, the team was in seven playoffs but did not win a division or conference title. However, after a series of unfortunate incidents during the late 1990s and early 2000s, the Hornets' popularity declined and so did their attendances in games at the Coliseum.

When a nonbinding public referendum that included building the team a new arena using taxpayer money failed, franchise owner George Shinn received permission from NBA officials to relocate it somewhere else. After evaluating the economic benefits and costs of sites in Louisville, Norfolk, St. Louis, and other cities, Shinn moved his team in 2002 from North Carolina to Louisiana and renamed it New Orleans Hornets.[5]

Since the 2002–2003 NBA season, the Hornets–renamed Pelicans in 2013–have been in five playoffs and won a division title in 2008. For some recent but good news off the court, Tom Benson, who also owns the NFL New Orleans Saints, purchased the franchise for $338 million. When he became owner, Benson signed a long-term lease with the City of New Orleans and said he preferred a new name for his team that represented something local to New Orleans given Louisiana's state bird, the Brown Pelican. In addition, Benson received even better news by winning the first overall pick in the NBA lottery. As such, the club became the Pelicans and drafted former University of Kentucky All-American Anthony Davis. Because of his rebounding and scoring in games, 6-ft.–10-in. forward/center Davis was on the league's 2014 WC all-star team.

In retrospect, the Pelicans opened their 2013–2014 NBA season with a new name, renovated arena, and a franchise record for season ticket sales. More specifically, the New Orleans Arena underwent the first stage of a publicly funded $50 million facelift. Because of work on the arena's club and suite levels, the team expects to generate at least $5 million more a year from these changes.

Furthermore, franchise owner Tom Benson instituted dramatic price cuts to tickets in the 2013–2014 season to stem low attendance, which was the NBA's second worst during 2012–2013 at just 13,803 per game. The result of reducing prices was roughly 12,000 season ticket sales compared to 11,800 when the team won a franchise-record 56 games during the 2007–2008 NBA season.

---

[5]Various articles highlight different aspects about the Hornets' move from Charlotte in 2002 and the club's opportunities and problems in New Orleans. These include "Hornets, City Officials Agree to Win-Win Practice Site Deal," *New Orleans CityBusiness* (24 January 2005), 26; Jere Longman, "Hornets Thrive Amid Empty Seats in New Orleans," *New York Times* (12 February 2008), 1; Jack McCallum, "Hello, New Orleans," *Sports Illustrated* (11 November 2002), 76; Irwin Speizer, "Shinn Given City a Surprise Boost," *Business North Carolina* (December 2002), 10; "The Buzzing Sound," *New Orleans CityBusiness* (21 January 2002), 26; Liz Robbins, "Traveling Music For the Hornets," *New York Times* (7 July 2002), 6; "Charlotte Bidders Are Heard," *New York Times* (17 December 2002), D6.

Seattle Supersonics → Oklahoma City Thunder

An NBA expansion team in 1967, the Supersonics competed against others for 41 seasons in the league. During this period, the club was in 21 playoffs and won six division and three conference titles, and an NBA championship in 1979. Some of its most productive players included guards Gus Williams, Nate McMillan, Lenny Wilkins, and Fred Brown; forward Spencer Haywood; and center Jack Sikma.

For business and personal reasons, the Supersonics' owners sold their franchise in 2006 for $350 million to a group of investors led by entrepreneur Clay Bennett. Shortly thereafter, Bennett negotiated with Seattle government officials to construct a new arena for his team financed with public money or alternatively, to significantly renovate the city's 13-year-old, 17,000-seat Key Arena. When Bennett's efforts failed, the NBA authorized him to relocate his team in 2008 from the State of Washington to Oklahoma and rename it the Oklahoma City Thunder.[6]

In two regular seasons, the Thunder won 43 games or 26 % of them. Then from 2010 to 2013, the team was in four playoffs and won three division and one conference title primarily because of high scoring Kevin Durant and point guard Russell Westbrook. In the league's 2013–2014 regular season, the Thunder had the WC's highest winning percentage and motivated enough to compete for an NBA championship barring injuries to Durant and Westbrook.

During the NBA's 2012–2013 season, the Thunder had the league's top television ratings on Fox Sports Oklahoma. In fact, they were triple the rating of the previous season. This, in part, reflects a relatively small sports market's love affair with a professional basketball team that moved from Seattle in 2008 and won three consecutive division titles.

Since February 2011, the Thunder has sold out every game at the 18,203-seat Chesapeake Energy Arena with 4,000 people on a season ticket waiting list. In addition, the team raised ticket prices for the 2013–2014 NBA season, which was the first increase for more than half of season ticket holders since the team arrived in Oklahoma City. Even better, all-star forward/center Kevin Durant is under contract through the league's 2015–2016 season. From a financial perspective, the franchise has an opportunity to prosper in 2015 and in years thereafter.

---

[6] To read more about the Supersonics move to Oklahoma City, see "Deal Allows the Sonics to Leave Seattle For Oklahoma City," *New York Times* (3 July 2008), 6; Richard Sandomir, "Sonics Given Approval to Move to Oklahoma," *New York Times* (19 April 2008), 2; "Sonics' Bid to Leave Seattle Gets League Nod," *Wall Street Journal* (21 April 2008), A10; "Sonics the Most Likely to Move," *Charlotte Observer* (19 February 2006), 14C; Howard Bloom, "Welcome to Franchise Relocation Hell——the Seattle Sonics" at http://www.sportsbusinessnews.com cited 5 November 2007; Jim Cour, "Sonics Looking at Arena Alternatives" at http://www.netscape.sports.com cited 1 February 2006.

New Jersey Nets → Brooklyn Nets

An original member of the ABA in 1967, the Nets was initially the New Jersey Americans. One year later, the team moved to Long Island and played in various arenas there as the New York Nets. Led by Hall of Famer Julius Erving, the Nets won two ABA championships before becoming one of four ABA teams admitted into the NBA as part of the league's merger in 1976. Then in 1977, the team moved from New York back to New Jersey and became the New Jersey Nets.

During their 35 years in New Jersey, the Nets experienced periods of losing and misfortune intermittent with several periods of success, which culminated in NBA Final appearances in the 2001–2002 and 2002–2003 seasons. However, after appearing in consecutive playoffs from 2002 to 2007, winning four division and two conference titles but no league championships, things got worse for the Nets as they became the sole tenant in the Meadowlands because the NHL Devils had completed their move to the Newark Arena. At the same time, lawsuits continued to hold up an arena project that would take the Nets from New Jersey to Brooklyn, New York.

After numerous delays to the project, Russian billionaire Mikhail Prokhorov agreed to a $200 million deal in September 2009 to become principal owner of the Nets and a key investor in their proposed home in Brooklyn. Indeed, he provided funding for the new arena and thereby its eventual construction. After the dismissal of major pending lawsuits, groundbreaking for the $1 billion, 17,732-seat Barclays Center occurred during March 2010. In September 2011, celebrity entertainer and Nets minority owner Jay-Z announced that the team's new name after moving to Brooklyn would be the Brooklyn Nets, which became official in April 2012.

After losing to the Chicago Bulls in the 2013 playoffs, the Nets fired head coach P.J. Carlisemo and hired Jason Kidd who had recently retired after a 19-year career and playing for the New York Knicks in his final season. Kidd named Lawrence Frank as his assistant coach, looking to learn on the job from the coach who was there for most of Kidd's tenure in New Jersey. The Nets also brought in three veterans with a champion pedigree when they acquired Paul Pierce, Kevin Garnett, and Jason Terry in addition to D.J. White in a blockbuster trade with the Boston Celtics.

Regarding business deals, Mikhail Prokhorov invested $293 million during May 2010 for an 80 % interest in the Nets; a 45 % stake in the Brooklyn Arena's Limited Liability Corporation (LLC), which is the operating company that controls the team's new building; and up to 20 % in the Atlantic Yards Development's LLC, which will develop real estate near the new Barclays Center arena. Because of these deals, *Forbes* estimated that the enterprise value for the team and arena was $365 million.

After moving into their state-of-the art facility in 2012, the Nets expected to earn sponsorship, premium seating, and concession revenues of $75 million per year, which is $60 million more than what the team received at the Izod Center the previous NBA season. In addition, annual debt service on the new building, which the franchise financed with $511 million in Pilot bonds, will be between $27 million and $30 million.

For the 2013–2014 NBA season, franchise owner Mikhail Prokhorov adopted a player payroll of $101 million, which carried a luxury tax bill of more than $80 million. Even with an extended playoff run, the Nets will probably lose at least $50 million. According to Pollstar, the Barclays Center was the busiest arena in America during the first 6 months of 2013 with the sale of 657,423 tickets. The only venues in the world that outsold Barclays in ticket sales were the O2 and Manchester Arena in England.

Table 5.2 contains financial information about seven NBA teams in this chapter. Grouped, their average estimated market value in 2013 was $556 million, revenue $135 million, operating income $11 million, and player expenses $74 million. The Nets had the highest amounts in three types of data while the lowest in value were the Pelicans, in revenue and player expenses the Kings, and in operating income the Nets.

For how their amounts compared to those of other NBA teams in 2013, the New York Knicks ranked highest in value at $1.4 billion and Milwaukee Bucks lowest at $405 million; Los Angeles Lakers first in revenue at $287 million and Bucks thirtieth at $109 million; Knicks highest in operating income at $96 million and Brooklyn Nets lowest at –$19 million; and Miami Heat third in player expenses at $90 million and Sacramento Kings thirtieth at $61 million. Based on information in the table, the Nets, Clippers, and Thunder had the most impressive data while the Pelicans, Grizzlies, and Kings were worst in the group from a financial perspective.

With respect to these seven teams' number of NBA seasons and their playoffs and championships before and after they relocated, there were different results. For example, as of 2013, four or 44 % of them played more seasons before than after

Table 5.2 Seven NBA teams, 2013 financial data

Team	Value (Rank)	Revenue	Operating income	Player expenses
Brooklyn Nets	780 (5)	190	–19	94
Los Angeles Clippers	575 (13)	128	15	80
Memphis Grizzlies	453 (24)	126	11	71
New Orleans Pelicans	420 (28)	116	11	70
Oklahoma City Thunder	590 (11)	144	33	74
Sacramento Kings	550 (16)	115	12	61
Utah Jazz	525 (17)	131	17	74

Note: NBA is National Basketball Association. Amounts are in millions. Rank is among 30 NBA teams. Revenue and operating income are for the 2012–2013 season and net of revenue sharing and arena debt service. Value is an estimate based on teams' current arena deal (unless new arena is pending) without deduction for debt (other than arena debt). Revenue is net of arena revenues used for debt payments. Operating income is earnings before interest, taxes, depreciation, and amortization. Player expenses include benefits and bonuses

Source: Kurt Badenhausen, Michael Ozanian, and Christina Settimi, "NBA Team Values: The Business of Basketball" at http://www.forbes.com cited 6 February 2014

they moved including the former Buffalo Braves, Charlotte Hornets, Seattle Supersonics, and New Jersey Nets. While the San Diego Clippers discontinued operations in 1984, it will be 34 years when the Brooklyn Nets exceed their predecessor and 36 years when the Thunder surpasses the Supersonics in number of seasons at their home sites (Table A5.1).

Regarding their playoffs, 5 or 55 % of them qualified for more postseasons after relocating to their new sites. In other words, the New Jersey Nets, Utah Jazz, Los Angeles Clippers, Sacramento Kings, and Memphis Grizzlies performed better during more regular seasons than before in, respectively, New York, New Orleans, San Diego, Kansas City, and Vancouver.

For championships won while at premove and postmove sites, the number of them increased from 17 to 24. Five teams won more championships after relocating, two had fewer of them, and another two had zero at both their premove and postmove sites. Furthermore, as of the 2012–2013 NBA season, the Clippers, Kings, and Hornets/Pelicans won one more division title while located in, respectively, Los Angeles, Sacramento, and New Orleans. In short, the majority of team relocations from 1977 to 2012 were more successful for the league, franchise owners, and communities from business, competitive, and/or economics perspectives.[7]

In Table A5.2 are the population and population ranks of metropolitan areas for teams before and subsequent to their relocation. Except for the Buffalo Braves to San Diego in 1978, San Diego Clippers to Los Angeles in 1984, and New Jersey Nets to Brooklyn in 2012, the other clubs moved their operations from larger to smaller metropolitan areas. This occurred for several reasons. First, sports fans in such markets as New Orleans, Kansas City, and Vancouver did not attend local NBA games because their hometown team performed poorly against others in the league.

Second, some teams moved to play their home games in a new or renovated arena. For example, the Barclays Center opened for the Nets in 2012. As a result, amenities at this attractive, expensive, and modern facility will increase the Nets' attendances and thus its gate receipts, revenues, and profits, and furthermore, allow the club to expand players' payroll to become more competitive in the Eastern Conference's Atlantic Division in future seasons.

Third, a few franchises were sold to a different ownership group affiliated in some way with another city. Unable to survive financially at its current arena and to negotiate a new lease, the new owners evaluated other sites and received approval from the league to move their team to another area.

Fourth, there were no MLB or NFL teams in places like Salt Lake City, Sacramento, Memphis, and Oklahoma City. Consequently, fans there would likely support an NBA franchise. In addition, some local businesses in these cities might

---

[7] Besides such NBA teams as the Sacramento Kings, Charlotte Hornets, and Seattle Supersonics, interesting data about them and others and their histories are in Connie Kirchberg, *Hoop Love: A History of the National Basketball Association* (Jefferson, NC: McFarland, 2007); Leonard Koppett, *Total Basketball: The Ultimate Basketball Encyclopedia* (Wilmington, DE: Sport Classic Books, 2004); Robert W. Peterson, *Cages to Jump Shots: Pro Basketball's Early Years* (New York, NY: Oxford University Press, 1990); Kyle Wright, *The NBA From Top to Bottom: A History of the NBA, From the No. 1 Team Through No. 1,153* (Bloomington, IN: iUniverse, Inc., 2007).

have the resources to become partners and sponsors, and provide additional revenue for a professional basketball team.

This concludes the discussion of why, when, and where nine NBA teams moved their operations to other places before a league merger in 1976. In Chap. 5 is an overview of team movements from 1976 to 2013 and whether these were the optimal economic decisions for communities, franchises owners, and the NBA.[8]

[8] Some additional information about these teams and their relocation is in "Basketball History" at http://www.history-of-basketball.com cited 20 September 2005; "History of Basketball" at http://library.thinkquest.org cited 24 August 2009; "National Basketball Association (NBA) History" at http://www.rauzulusstreet.com cited 12 August 2005; "NBA Growth Timetable" at http://www.basketball.com cited 17 September 2005; "Professional Basketball Leagues" at http://apbr.org cited 22 August 2009. For current literature, see the *Official NBA Guide*: *2013–14 Edition* (New York, NY: NBA Properties, 2013), and *Official NBA Register*: *2013–14 Edition* (New York, NY: NBA Properties, 2013).

Part III
League Mergers

Chapter 6
National Basketball League–Basketball Association of America

Prior to the late 1930s, two basketball leagues emerged and their teams had operations at sites in small, midsized, and large cities of the United States (US). These were the National Basket Ball League (NBBL), which existed from 1898 to 1904, and the American Basketball League (ABL) during 1925–1955.[1]

After a few regular seasons, the NBBL failed because of financial and organizational problems, poor decision-making by league administrators, lack of support from local businesses, low number of spectators at home and away games, and in general, teams' performances for a small number of basketball fans in relatively minor sports markets. Although the ABL had some clubs playing their games in arenas and gymnasiums located in midsized and large metropolitan areas, the league folded in 1955 after completing 25 seasons. That was due, in part, to selfish sports franchise owners and talented but low-paid players who frequently left their ABL team and joined others in different professional or semiprofessional basketball leagues. Alternatively, some players simply entered the military to serve in World War II, obtained jobs in businesses, or became public employees.

To meet the gradual but increasing market demand for professional team sports and create a permanent league that had economic power and entertained fans at teams' games in cities across the US, two American professional basketball

[1] The NBBL was the first professional basketball league in the world. Centered in Philadelphia, Pennsylvania, the league's teams stretched from New York City to Central New Jersey and throughout the Philadelphia area to Wilmington, Delaware. It began operations with the 1898–1999 season and disbanded in January 1904, which was prior to completing its 1903–1904 season. Originally intended to consist of two separate geographic districts, one based in Philadelphia and the other in New York City, the latter district never operated. During the off-season in 1903, the NBBL had problems. Only five teams elected to play and more importantly, teams in New York, Burlington, and Wilmington failed to return. The league began the season with only five teams—Camden Electrics, Trenton Potters, Conshohocken, Millville Glass Blowers, and St. Bridget's Biddies. Later, the Electrics and Potters dropped out in December 1903. Subsequently, the league disbanded in 1904 and at least one lawsuit followed its demise. See John Grasso, *Historical Dictionary of Basketball* (Lanham, MD: Scarecrow Press, 2011).

F.P. Jozsa Jr., *National Basketball Association Strategies*,
SpringerBriefs in Economics 84, DOI 10.1007/978-3-319-10058-6_6

organizations consolidated their operations in 1949. This chapter describes each organization's history and then discusses the formation of the National Basketball Association (NBA). In addition, tables provide information about these leagues' teams and their competitiveness and development for 1 or more years.

History

National Basketball League

The Midwest Basketball Conference, which opened in 1935, changed its name 2 years later to the National Basketball League (NBL) in order to expand geographically into other cities and thereby attract larger audiences to teams' games. Interestingly, some entrepreneurial executives in the General Electric, Firestone, and Goodyear companies, who loved sports, made plans and had the determination, financial support, and initiative to organize the league.[2]

For the most part, the NBL consisted of small market and corporate teams from the Great Lakes region with the majority of them based at sites in Illinois, Indiana, Michigan, New York, Ohio, Pennsylvania, and Wisconsin. Beginning informally in 1937, the league started with 13 previously independent teams. According to NBL rules, scheduling games was the responsibility of each team who had to perform in at least ten of them including four on the road. For each game, the home team decided either to play four 10-min quarters or three 15-min periods. Although teams were competitors, companies who owned them found jobs for their players.

The NBL's history had three distinct eras, each contributing significantly to the growth of professional basketball across the US and then establishment of the NBA in 1949. While the first dynasties were the Oshkosh All-Stars, the middle years focused on the emergence of the Fort Wayne Zollner Pistons, who later were instrumental in the survival of the NBA during its infancy. In the NBL's final years, the important subject was the Minneapolis Lakers' George Mikan and emergence of big, tall, and strong athletes in professional basketball.

During the first era, the Oshkosh All-Stars, who appeared in the championship series five consecutive years (1938–1942) and won two titles, were outstanding because of rugged 6-ft.–4-in. center Leroy "Cowboy" Edwards. Besides being a most valuable player (MVP), he led the NBL in scoring from 1937 to 1940 with, respectively, 16.2, 11.9, and 12.9 points-per-game (ppg). Other outstanding players for the All-Stars were Bob Carpenter, Gene Englund, and Charlie Shipp. In addition

[2]According to Murray R. Nelson, who wrote *The National Basketball League: A History, 1935–1949*, the league originally formed in Akron and Indianapolis, operated mainly in the Midwest but extended as far east as Rochester and Syracuse and west to Denver, and established major franchises with hometown loyalties. Most of its star players were college graduates, a major change from previous professional leagues. In addition, it was the first modern major professional league to integrate.

to its NBL titles, the team also won the 1942 World Professional Basketball Tournament by defeating the Detroit Eagles in Chicago.

Regarding the NBL's middle years, the Fort Wayne Zollner Pistons–so nicknamed because industrialist Fred Zollner owned them and his company manufactured pistons for engines–were led by tough veteran Bobby McDermott. In fact, the team finished second in 1942 and 1943 and then won league title in 1944 and 1945. Similar to many professional basketball teams, the Pistons frequently played their games in armories, ballrooms, and high school gymnasiums.

While owned by Zollner, the Pistons eventually played an important role in the survival and growth of the NBA. In fact, Zollner's financial support helped the league stay afloat during its tumultuous formative years. Challenging the Zollner Pistons for supremacy were the Sheboygan Redskins. Beginning in the season before Fort Wayne joined the NBL, the Redskins appeared in five championship series in six seasons. They lost to Oshkosh in the 1941 finals and beat the Pistons for the title in 1943 but lost to them in 1944 and 1945. One year later, Sheboygan lost in the finals to the league's newest member, the powerhouse Rochester Royals, who boasted such Hall of Fame players as Al Cervi, Bob Davies, and Red Holzman.

Featured in the NBL's third era was 6-ft.–10-in. George Mikan, a three-time All-American center from DePaul University who became the dominant player in the sport. As a rookie, Mikan led the Chicago American Gears to the 1947 NBL title but before the next season, owner Maurice White pulled his team out of the league and formed his own 24-team circuit called the Professional Basketball League of America (PBLA). After that venture failed, the NBL's Minneapolis Lakers signed Mikan, who with versatile forward Jim Pollard won the league's 1948 championship.

After their 1947–1948 season ended, the Lakers and three other NBL clubs left to join the Basketball Association of America (BAA). Stripped of its best teams and prime gate attractions, the NBL lasted one more season when the Anderson Duffey Packers defeated the Oshkosh All-Stars in three games and won the league's last championship.

When one of its replacement clubs folded, the NBL added an all-black team in December of its final season (1948–1949). Named the Detroit Vagabond Kings, the league originally awarded the franchise to a famous African American barnstorming team, the New York Rens, to play out the season in Dayton, Ohio as the Dayton Rens. Meanwhile, the rival BAA had only white players and later the NBA was an all-white league for one season before integrating in 1950.

For sure, the NBL contributed significantly to the formation of the NBA but also had major accomplishments in other ways, most notably in offering opportunities for African American players. For example, with many athletes serving in the armed forces, the NBL's Toledo Jim White Chevrolets and Chicago Studebaker Flyers filled their rosters by signing African Americans in the league's 1942–1943 season, which was 4 years before Jackie Robinson broke professional baseball's color barrier with the Brooklyn Dodgers.

When the Chevrolets signed several black players to start the season, including former University of Toledo all-star Bill Jones, the team lost its first four games and folded due to financial difficulties. Furthermore, the Studebaker Flyers stocked their roster with several members of the Harlem Globetrotters who worked at the company's factory, but they also folded after compiling an 8–15 record.

Regarding its other milestones, the NBL helped to create the Indianapolis Olympians for the 1949–1950 NBA season. When the NBL and BAA merged in 1949, the Olympians, without playing any games, joined the NBA to replace the Indianapolis Jets. Leading the Olympians were University of Kentucky alumni Alex Groza and Ralph Beard, both of whom were key contributors on the 1948 gold medalist US Olympic basketball team. However, after the 1951 season, NBA President Maurice Podoloff suspended Groza and Beard for life when they admitted to point shaving during their college careers. The Olympians finished with a 28–43 record in 1953 and 1 year later, went bankrupt and folded their operation.

Five former NBA teams trace their history to the NBL and its regular seasons. These were the Anderson Duffey Packers in 1946–1949, Denver Nuggets in 1948–1949, Indianapolis Kautskys in 1937–1948, Sheboygan Redskins in 1938–1949, and Waterloo Hawks in 1948–1949. While the Jets played in the BAA's 1948–1949 season, the remaining teams did so in the NBA's 1949–1950 season. Later, the Duffey Packers (aka Anderson Packers), Redskins, and Hawks joined the National Professional Basketball League (NPBL) in 1950.

In retrospect, five current NBA teams trace their history to the NBL. Three NBL teams joined the BAA in 1948 including the Minneapolis Lakers (now Los Angeles Lakers), Rochester Royals (now Sacramento Kings), and Fort Wayne Zollner Pistons (now Detroit Pistons). Besides them, two more NBL teams joined the NBA in 1949. These were the Buffalo Bisons/Tri-Cities Blackhawks (now Atlanta Hawks) and Syracuse Nationals (now Philadelphia 76ers).

An NBL franchise that continued to operate for decades was the Akron Goodyear Wingfoots, who won a league championship in 1938. The Wingfoots suspended operations during World War II and thus were not a part of the BAA/NBL merger. Instead, they remained in the National Industrial Professional League (NIPL), which in 1961 became the National AAU Basketball League (NABL). The Wingfoots were an elite team in the NABL.

Table 6.1 contains some historical but interesting information about all NBL teams. The most successful of them are those that joined the NBA in 1949 and then those who played in other professional basketball leagues such as the Akron Goodyear Wingfoots, Chicago American Gears, and Fort Wayne General Electrics. Meanwhile, the others disbanded, merged, or became barnstorming teams.

In short, the NBL was an effort to launch a new league of mostly corporate teams primarily at sites in small sports markets across the US. Despite its failure in the late 1940s, the NBL paved the way for the NBA to officially operate as a professional league in 1949 and continue to exist and become more popular and prosperous in decades thereafter.

Table 6.1 NBL teams, league historical information, 1937–1948 seasons

Team	Seasons	Championships	History
Akron Firestone Non-Skids	4	2	Disbanded in 1941
Akron Goodyear Wingfoots	5	1	Joined NIBL in 1947
Anderson Duffey Packers	3	1	Joined NBA in 1949
Buffalo Bisons	0	0	Moved to Tri-Cities in 1946
Chicago American Gears	3	1	Joined PBLA in 1947
Chicago Bruins	3	0	Disbanded in 1942
Chicago Studebaker Flyers	1	0	Disbanded in 1943
Cincinnati Comellos	1	0	Disbanded in 1938
Cleveland Chase Brassmen	1	0	Disbanded in 1944
Cleveland Allmen Transfers	2	0	Disbanded in 1946
Cleveland White Horses	1	0	Disbanded in 1939
Columbus Athletic Supply	1	0	Disbanded in 1939
Dayton Metropolitans	1	0	Disbanded in 1938
Dayton Rens	1	0	Disbanded in 1949
Denver Nuggets	1	0	Joined NBA in 1949
Detroit Eagles	2	0	Barnstorming team in 1941
Detroit Gems	1	0	Disbanded in 1947
Detroit Vagabond Kings	0	0	Disbanded in 1948
Flint/Midland Dow A.C.'s	1	0	Disbanded in 1948
Fort Wayne General Electrics	1	0	Joined NIBL in 1947
Fort Wayne Zollner Pistons	7	2	Joined BAA in 1948
Hammond Ciesar All-Americans	3	0	Disbanded in 1941
Hammond Calumet Buccaneers	1	0	Disbanded in 1949
Indianapolis Kautskys	11	0	Joined BAA in 1948
Kankakee Gallagher Trojans	1	0	Disbanded in 1938
Minneapolis Lakers	1	1	Joined BAA in 1948
Oshkosh All-Stars	12	2	Disbanded in 1949
Pittsburgh Pirates	2	0	Inactivated 1940–1943
Pittsburgh Raiders	1	0	Disbanded in 1945
Richmond King Clothiers	0	0	Became Cincinnati Comellos
Rochester Royals	3	1	Joined BAA in 1948
Sheboygan Redskins	11	1	Joined NBA in 1949
Syracuse Nationals	3	0	Joined NBA in 1949
Toledo Jim White Chevrolets	2	0	Disbanded in 1943
Toledo Jeeps	2	0	Disbanded in 1948
Tri-Cities Blackhawks	3	0	Joined NBA in 1949
Warren Penns	1	0	Moved to Cleveland in 1938
Waterloo Hawks	1	0	Joined NBA in 1949
Whiting Ciesar All-Americans	1	0	Moved to Hammond in 1938
Youngstown Bears	2	0	Disbanded in 1947

Note: Abbreviations represent National Basketball League (NBL), National Industrial Basketball League (NIBL), Professional Basketball League of America (PBLA), NBA, and Basketball Association of America (BAA). Some teams did not play entire seasons including the Buffalo Bisons, Detroit Vagabond Kings, and Richmond King Clothiers

Source: James Quirk and Rodney D. Fort, *Pay Dirt*: *The Business of Professional Team Sports* (Princeton, NJ: Princeton University Press, 1992); Frank P. Jozsa Jr., *The National Basketball Association*: *Business*, *Organization and Strategy* (Singapore: World Scientific, 2011); Murray R. Nelson, *The National Basketball League*: *A History*, *1935–1949* (Jefferson, NC: McFarland, 2009); "National Basketball League (NBL) Teams" at http://www.rauzulusstreet.com cited 31 July 2009

Basketball Association of America

During June 1944, a group of New York City business executives founded the BAA while meeting at the city's Commodore Hotel, which was next to Grand Central Station. Simply put, their goal was to find a way to make basketball arenas more profitable in the fall and winter months.

The group, which consisted of such innovators as Boston Garden manager Walter Brown, Cleveland Arena owner Al Sutphin, and Madison Square Garden president Ned Irish, chose American Hockey League President Maurice Podoloff to operate their organization. Although Podoloff knew very little about the game and business of basketball, his knowledge of law and real estate was sufficient for them to appoint him. In addition, the group picked sports media specialist and future NBA commissioner Walter Kennedy to market and promote the BAA.

In 1946, the BAA granted charters to 11 franchises. Located primarily at sites in midsized-to-large cities of populated metropolitan areas, their teams played a schedule of 60, 48-min games each in the regular season. However, despite the size and location of their sports markets, some BAA clubs failed to establish an identity, image, and likeability with their hometown fans. Moreover, potential troubles for the BAA were college basketball doubleheaders being popular sports events, talented athletes performing for teams in the NBL and industrial leagues, and some arenas in cities not available to host games of BAA clubs.

The new league opened in November 1946 with teams in 11 cities. In the Eastern Division (ED) were the Washington Capitols, Philadelphia Warriors, New York Knickerbockers, Providence Steamrollers, Boston Celtics, and Toronto Huskies. Meanwhile, the Western Division (WD) included the Chicago Stags, St. Louis Bombers, Cleveland Rebels, Detroit Falcons, and Pittsburgh Ironmen. In the championship series, the ED Warriors beat the WD Stags in five games and won the BAA's first title (Table 6.2).

Because of economic and other problems, four original BAA teams folded in 1947 due to internal conflicts while the ABL's Baltimore Bullets joined the league that season. With physically tough players who used rugged tactics and a slowdown type of offense in their games, the WD Bullets became a league champion by defeating the ED Warriors in six games despite the reduction of regular season games from 60 in 1946 to 48 in 1947.

During various professional basketball teams' first year in venues shared with ice hockey clubs, some arena owners simply put a wooden basketball floor over the ice. This caused some BAA games to cancel due to puddles of water on the floor. In addition, some arena owners would not heat their buildings causing fans to bring blankets to the games and players to wear gloves. While attendances averaged about 3,000 per game, BAA teams with large leads stalled by having players dribble the ball for long periods. Meanwhile, team owners even discussed "innings" in which each club had the ball for a specific time period. Although several clubs were financially weak and not competitive, the BAA still had fans eager to see former college stars perform in games.

Table 6.2 BAA teams, league historical information, 1946–1948 seasons

Team	BAA seasons	BAA championships	History
Baltimore Bullets	2	1	Joined NBA in 1949
Boston Celtics	3	0	Joined NBA in 1949
Chicago Stags	3	0	Joined NBA in 1949
Cleveland Rebels	1	0	Disbanded in 1947
Detroit Falcons	1	0	Disbanded in 1947
Fort Wayne Pistons	1	0	Joined NBA in 1949
Indianapolis Jets	1	0	Disbanded in 1949
Minneapolis Lakers	1	1	Joined NBA in 1949
New York Knickerbockers	3	0	Joined NBA in 1949
Philadelphia Warriors	3	1	Joined NBA in 1949
Pittsburgh Ironmen	1	0	Disbanded in 1947
Providence Steamrollers	3	0	Disbanded in 1949
Rochester Royals	1	0	Joined NBA in 1949
St. Louis Bombers	3	0	Joined NBA in 1949
Toronto Huskies	1	0	Disbanded in 1947
Washington Capitols	3	0	Joined NBA in 1949

Note: BAA is Basketball Association of America. Number of BAA seasons and championships are teams' during the 1946–1947 to 1948–1949 seasons. Championships include division titles and league championships

Source: "BAA Teams" at http://www.nbahoopsonline.com cited 3 March 2014

Prior to the 1948–1949 season in professional basketball, the NBL's Fort Wayne Pistons, Indianapolis Kautskys (renamed Jets), Minneapolis Lakers, and Rochester Royals joined the BAA. This caused a surge in talent because such players as the Lakers' George Mikan now played in the BAA, which became two 6-team divisions with each team playing 60 regular season games.

The BAA's 1949 playoffs expanded to include eight teams. The four best teams from the ED and WD competed in divisional semifinals and then finals to find each division's winner. The two division winners then advanced to the league finals. The divisional semifinals and finals were in a best-of-3 format while the final series consisted of best-of-7 format. The Lakers defeated the Royals and became the inaugural WD winner. In the other divisional final, the Capitols defeated the Knickerbockers to become the inaugural ED winner. Then, the Lakers won the finals by defeating the Capitols in six games. Thus, from 1947 to 1949, the Warriors, Bullets, and Lakers were champions beating, respectively, the Stags, Warriors, and Capitols.

Although economically weak but temporarily viable as a business organization, the BAA finished its regular season schedule of games and successfully concluded the 1948–1949 postseason. Even so, it was apparent to BAA President Podoloff and Public Relations Director Kennedy that sports fans responded more to former players from the NBL who performed on current BAA teams. Nevertheless, BAA clubs played in the sport's best arenas and furthermore, they existed within markets with midsized-to-large populations.

BAA–NBL Merger

In August 1949, the BAA agreed to absorb the NBL and that led to the eventual creation of the NBA. Consequently, the six remaining NBL teams–Anderson Duffey Packers, Denver Nuggets, Sheboygan Redskins, Syracuse Nationals, Tri-Cities Blackhawks, and Waterloo Hawks–gained admission into the BAA, which then had ten teams after the BAA's Indianapolis Jets and Providence Steamrollers disbanded following the 1948–1949 season. The Indianapolis Olympians, which was a planned expansion team of the NBL, replaced the Jets and then joined the newly formed NBA.

In total, the new organization had 17 teams located in various small, midsized, and large cites of US metropolitan areas, and who played their home and/or away games in big arenas, average sized gymnasiums, and tiny armories. Prior to the merger, the BAA held its 1949 College Draft, which was the league's last event.

With respect to the former NBL and BAA teams, they had different seasons and some were more active, prosperous, and successful than others while playing in regular seasons and postseasons of the NBA. This section contains information about them and their histories from 1949–1950 to the 2012–2013 season. The list of teams, however, excludes the Indianapolis Olympians who replaced the Indianapolis Jets in 1949 and thus did not perform in any regular seasons or postseasons of the NBL or BAA (Table 6.3).[3]

Anderson Packers

Based in Anderson, Indiana, the Packers were the property of brothers John and Ike Duffey who operated Duffey Farms Inc., a local meatpacking company. John was president of the club and Ike its secretary-treasurer. The brothers profitably sold their Anderson plant in 1949 although they retained ownership of the team until its demise.

After playing in the NBL from 1946 to 1949, the team joined the NBA before the 1949–1950 season and qualified for but defeated in the league's playoffs. The franchise withdrew from the NBA during April 1950 and then moved to the NPBL, which folded in 1951.

[3] One year after moving from the NBL to BAA in 1948, the Indianapolis Jets withdrew and the Indianapolis Olympians replaced them to compete in the NBA's 1949–1950 regular season. The team played four seasons in the league and competed in four divisional playoffs. In 1951, the team's owners became involved in a game-throwing scandal that occurred years earlier while playing at the University of Kentucky. Three years later, the Olympians went bankrupt and cancelled the franchise before the NBA's 1954–1955 season.

Table 6.3 Former NBL and BAA teams, historical information, since 1949–1950 NBA season

Team (former league)	NBA seasons	Championships	History
Anderson Packers (NBL)	1	0	Joined NPBL in 1950
Baltimore Bullets (BAA)	5	0	Disbanded in 1954
Boston Celtics (BAA)	65	68	Current team
Chicago Stags (BAA)	1	1	Disbanded in 1950
Denver Nuggets (NBL)	1	0	Disbanded in 1950
Fort Wayne Pistons (BAA)	8	2	Moved to Detroit in 1957
Minneapolis Lakers (BAA)	11	8	Moved to Los Angeles in 1960
New York Knicks (BAA)	65	18	Current team
Philadelphia Warriors (BAA)	13	2	Moved to San Francisco in 1962
Rochester Royals (BAA)	8	2	Moved to Cincinnati in 1957
Sheboygan Redskins (NBL)	1	0	Joined NPBL in 1950
St. Louis Bombers (BAA)	1	0	Disbanded in 1950
Syracuse Nationals (NBL)	14	4	Moved to Philadelphia in 1963
Tri-Cities Blackhawks (NBL)	2	0	Moved to Milwaukee in 1951
Washington Capitols (BAA)	2	0	Disbanded in 1951
Waterloo Hawks (NBL)	1	0	Joined NPBL in 1950

Note: The abbreviations represent National Basketball League (NBL), Basketball Association of America (BAA), National Basketball Association (NBA), and National Professional Basketball League (NPBL). Championships include NBA division and conference titles and league championships

Source: James Quirk and Rodney D. Fort, *Pay Dirt*: *The Business of Professional Team Sports* (Princeton, NJ: Princeton University Press, 1992), and Frank P. Jozsa Jr., *The National Basketball Association*: *Business, Organization and Strategy* (Singapore: World Scientific, 2011)

Baltimore Bullets

Before joining the NBA in 1949, the Baltimore Bullets played in the ABL from 1944 to 1947 and then in the BAA during the 1947–1948 and 1948–1949 seasons. Although the team won a BAA championship in 1948, it appeared in only one playoff series while in the NBA for five seasons. With a 3–11 record and low attendances at its home games, the Bullets folded their operations in November 1954 to become the last NBA franchise to fail. Of all defunct NBA teams, the Bullets were the only one to win a BAA championship.

Boston Celtics

A BAA team for three seasons, the Celtics franchise has been popular and successful since joining the NBA in 1949. Despite several changes in ownership during 65 seasons, the team was in 49 playoffs and won 30 division and 21 conference titles and 17 NBA championships. Indeed, such great coaches as Red Auerbach,

K.C. Jones, and Tom Heinsohn, and competitive players as guard Bob Cousy, center Bill Russell, and forward Larry Bird have led the Celtics in various seasons.[4]

Although the Celtics have not won a league championship since 2008, they appeared in two conference finals and one NBA final series. To win its division and challenge the Miami Heat, Indiana Pacers, and others for a conference title, the club needs a group of better players to replace the points scored and defensive excellence of former superstars Kevin Garnett and Paul Pierce. Former Butler University coach Brad Stevens is ambitious, smart, and young but requires more experience to be an effective leader of the Celtics in future seasons.

Chicago Stags

Owned by the Chicago Stadium Corporation, the Stags played in the BAA for 3 years. In their 1946–1947 season, the Stags won the WD but lost to the Philadelphia Warriors in the BAA finals. During the next season, they lost in the semifinals to the eventual champion Baltimore Bullets and in 1948–1949, finished third in their division but defeated by the champion Minneapolis Lakers in the playoffs.

In the 1949–1950 NBA season, the Stags tied for third in the Central Division (CD) with the Fort Wayne Pistons each with a 40–28 record. However, the team lost again to the Minneapolis Lakers in the division semifinals. This was the end of the NBA in northeast Illinois until the Chicago Packers became a franchise in 1961.

Denver Nuggets

Tracing their roots to 1932, the Nuggets were one of the most competitive and powerful nonprofessional basketball teams in the country, winning the 1939 Amateur Athletic Union (AAU) championship and losing the 1940 championship to the Phillips 66ers of Oklahoma. In 1948, the NBL awarded Denver, Colorado its first professional basketball franchise. The Nuggets' team in the 1948–1949 season included Morris Udall, who later served in the US House of Representatives from 1961 to 1991.

In 1949, the Nuggets joined the NBA. As the westernmost team in the league, the Nuggets played one season and finished with an 11–51 record and sixth in the WD. Within a year, the franchise cancelled its operations leaving Colorado without any major league sports teams until the birth of the American Football League Denver Broncos in 1960.

---

[4]Among NBA teams in 2013, the Celtics ranked fourth in estimated market value at $875 million, sixth in revenue at $169 million, fifth in operating income at $46.8 million, and eighth in player expenses at $79 million. For more details, see "NBA Team Values: The Business of Basketball" at http://www.forbes.com cited 12 February 2014.

Fort Wayne Pistons

While playing their home games in a gymnasium at Fort Wayne's North Side High School, the Zollner Pistons were NBL champions in 1944 and 1945 and won the World Professional Basketball Tournament from 1944 to 1946. Two years later, the team joined the BAA and changed its name to Fort Wayne Pistons.

After becoming an NBA franchise in 1949, the Pistons were in eight consecutive playoffs and won two division titles. There were rumors, however, that Pistons players conspired with gamblers to shave points and throw various games during the 1953–1954 and 1954–1955 seasons. Though the Pistons enjoyed support from many local sports fans, Fort Wayne's small population made it difficult for them to be profitable. Thus, owner Fred Zollner moved his team from Fort Wayne to Detroit in 1957.

Minneapolis Lakers

This franchise began to operate in 1947 when Minnesota entrepreneurs Ben Berger and Morris Chalfen purchased the recently disbanded Detroit Gems of the NBL for $15,000 and renamed them the Minneapolis Lakers. In their first season, they led the league with a 43–17 record and after moving from the NBL to BAA in 1948, won a championship by defeating the Washington Capitols four games to two. Following their 1948–1949 season, the Lakers joined the NBA.

Before moving to Los Angeles in 1960, the Lakers were in ten playoffs and won four each division titles and NBA championships. During that period, the team's greatest players were centers George Mikan and Clyde Lovellette, forwards Vern Mikklesen and Jim Pollard, and guard Slater Martin, each coached by John Kundla. When Mikan retired in 1956, the club's attendances at home declined causing financial problems. For the most part, this caused the franchise to relocate from the Midwest to the west coast.

New York Knicks

Since moving from the BAA to NBA in 1949, the Knicks were most successful in the late 1960s, early to mid-1970s, and early 1990s. During 65 seasons, the team qualified for 38 playoffs, won eight each division and conference titles, and league championships in 1970 and 1973. The club has several players in the Hall of Fame such as Dave DeBusschere, Jerry Lucas, Walt Frazier, Bill Bradley, and Willis Reed. They played on great Knicks teams in the 1960s and 1970s, and following them were point scorers like Bernard King, Bob McAdoo, and Patrick Ewing.

Playing their home games in New York City's Madison Square Garden, the Knicks have a large fan base and are a wealthy franchise. As reported in *Forbes* magazine, the team ranked first in the NBA with an estimated market value of $1.4

billion in 2013. In addition, the club earned $287 million in revenue and $96 million in operating income, and had $89 million in player expenses.

Despite superstar Carmelo Anthony, the Knicks underperformed in the 2013–2014 NBA season. To consistently win games and challenge the Boston Celtics, Brooklyn Nets, and other teams in the EC's Atlantic Division, Coach Mike Woodson needs more productivity from his starting players besides Anthony.

Philadelphia Warriors

Founded in 1946 as a charter member of the BAA, the Philadelphia Warriors won a championship in the league's inaugural 1946–1947 season. After moving from the BAA to the NBA in 1949, the team appeared in nine playoffs and won a division title and championship in 1956. In this era, the star players were Paul Arizin, Tom Gola, and Neil Johnston.

In 1959, the Warriors signed draft pick Wilt Chamberlain. Known as "Wilt the Stilt," he led the NBA in scoring seven times, shattered rebounding records, and forever changed professional basketball's style of play. During March 1962 at a Warriors home game played on a neutral court in Hershey, Pennsylvania, Chamberlain scored 100 points against the New York Knicks, which is a single-game record that ranks among the NBA's finest moments. After the 1961–1962 season, the team's new ownership group moved the franchise from Philadelphia to San Francisco.

Rochester Royals

One year after moving from the NBL to BAA in 1948, the Royals joined the NBA and played in the Central Division (CD) along with such teams as the Minneapolis Lakers and Fort Wayne Pistons. Despite their small arena and competitive schedule, the Royals finished no lower than second in their division from 1950 to 1955.

In 1951, the Royals won an NBA title, which is the only league championship in the franchise's history. When its roster turned over in 1955 and although moving into the Rochester War Memorial to play its home games, the NBA put pressure on owners Jack and Lester Harrison to sell or relocate their team to a larger city. Unable to make a profit in western New York, the club relocated from Rochester to Cincinnati in 1957.

Sheboygan Redskins

From the 1938 to 1948 NBL seasons, the Redskins were in four finals and won a league championship in 1943. Six years later, the team transferred from the NBL to BAA (renamed NBA) and finished the 1949–1950 season with a 22–40 record and 17 games behind the Indianapolis Olympians in the league's WD. Because of financial problems and sparse attendances at the city's Municipal Auditorium and Armory, the Redskins withdrew from the NBA in April 1950 and joined the new NPBL. Although the team had the league's best record in the 1950–1951 regular season, the NPBL dissolved and so did the Redskins in 1952.

St. Louis Bombers

After losing in the quarterfinals or semifinals during three BAA seasons, the Bombers joined the NBA in 1949. In that season, the team finished 26–42 and fifth in the CD, and thus did not qualify for the playoffs. Unable to attract fans to their games while having financial losses, the Bombers and five other teams dropped out of the league in 1950.

Syracuse Nationals

When the leagues merged in 1949, the Syracuse Nationals transferred from the NBL to NBA. From 1949 to 1963, the team was in 14 playoffs and besides four division titles won a league championship in 1955. During this period of NBA seasons, the club's best players were guard Hal Greer, center Earl Lloyd, and forward Dolph Schayes. Their coaches included Al Cervi, Paul Seymour, and Alex Hannum. After a syndicate purchased the team from franchise owner Danny Biasone in 1963, they moved the team from Syracuse to Philadelphia to fill a void left by the Philadelphia Warriors. In short, Syracuse was simply too small for the Nationals to be profitable and survive as the last small-town team in the league.

Tri-Cities Blackhawks

The Blackhawks, who played three seasons in the NBL, joined the NBA in 1949. Led by coach Red Auerbach, they finished their first NBA season with a 29–35 record and qualified for the league's 1950 playoffs. The following season, however, the Blackhawks finished last in the WD and missed the playoffs. By then, it was obvious that the Tri-Cities area of Moline and Rock Island, Illinois and Davenport, Iowa was an undersized sports market and unable to support an NBA team. In 1951, franchise owner Ben Kerner relocated his team to Milwaukee, Wisconsin.

Washington Capitols

Led by coach Red Auerbach and scorer Bob Feerick, the Washington Capitols were in three BAA playoffs from 1946 to 1949. The team then shifted from the BAA to NBA, had a 32–36 record in the league's 1949–1950 season, qualified for the playoffs, but lost in the ED semifinals. While playing its home games at the 7,500-seat Uline Arena, the Capitols folded in January 1951 with a 10–25 record and thus did not finish the regular season.

Waterloo Hawks

Founded in 1948, the team played in the NBL for one season and finished with a 30–32 record. After the BAA-NBL merger in 1949, the Hawks joined the NBA to become an original franchise in the league. In the 1949–1950 season, the team was 19–43 and fifth in the WD. Because of financial problems, the Hawks withdrew from the NBA in 1950 and played in the NPBL where it finished the season at 32–34. Although first in their division, the Hawks disbanded after the NPBL folded in 1951.

In Table A6.1 are the population and population ranks of city and metropolitan areas hosting teams in the BAA and NBL, who after they merged, formed the NBA in 1949 along with the Indianapolis Olympians. Except for Fort Wayne, the former BAA teams had sites in midsized to large sports markets particularly the New York Knickerbockers, Chicago Stags, and Philadelphia Warriors. Nevertheless, the Bullets, Stags, Pistons, Lakers, Royals, Bombers, and Capitols either folded or relocated to another city before the early 1960s. From the group of former BAA teams, the Celtics and Knickerbockers continued to operate through the NBA's 2013–2014 season.

Other than the Denver Nuggets and Syracuse Nationals, NBL teams played their home games at sites in very small markets as of 1949. Thus, they were not able to generate enough revenue to survive in the cities of Anderson, Indiana, or Sheboygan, Wisconsin, or Waterloo, Iowa, or in the Tri-Cities area of the Midwest. Besides them, the Nuggets failed in 1950 and the Nationals moved from Syracuse in 1963. Based on population data in the table, the majority of former BAA and NBL teams had little opportunity to exist for more than a few regular seasons after 1949.[5]

[5] For additional sources about the formation and early history of the NBA, see Frank P. Jozsa Jr., *The National Basketball Association: Business, Organization and Strategy* (Singapore: World Scientific, 2011); Connie Kirchberg, *Hoop Love: A History of the National Basketball Association* (Jefferson, NC: McFarland, 2007); Robert W. Peterson, *Cages to Jump Shots: Pro Basketball's Early Years* (New York, NY: Oxford University Press, 1990); Charles Rosen, *The First Tip-Off: The Incredible Story of the Birth of the NBA* (New York, NY: McGraw-Hill, 2008).

Chapter 7
American Basketball Association–National Basketball Association

History

American Basketball Association

Prior to the late 1960s, the Chicago Packers and Chicago Bulls were the only expansion teams that existed and played games in the National Basketball Association (NBA). Then in 1967–1968, the league approved the entry of such new teams as the San Diego Rockets, Seattle Supersonics, Milwaukee Bucks, and Phoenix Suns. In other words, because of substantial financial requirements and the NBA's failure to expand into other regions of the United States (US) besides the Midwest, southwest, and on the west coast, several sports markets in America were not home sites of elite professional basketball clubs.

Given this history and an opportunity to invade new markets, a group of investors including sports promoter Dennis Murphy and his partner attorney Gary Davidson organized the American Basketball Association (ABA) during the mid-to-late 1960s. In establishing, marketing, and promoting the ABA and scheduling regular season games for its teams, these entrepreneurs' goal was to offer a special and unique type of basketball for sports fans in contrast to the NBA.[1]

More specifically, the new league distinguished itself from its older counterpart by implementing a more wide-open, flashy style of offensive play including different rules such as a 30-s shot clock rather than the NBA's 24-s clock (although the ABA switched to the 24 s shot clock for the 1975–1976 season), and a three-point field goal. In addition, the ABA used a colorful red, white, and blue basketball instead of

[1] For more information about the league, see Terry Pluto, *Loose Balls*: *The Short*, *Wild Life of the American Basketball Association* (New York, NY: Simon & Schuster, 2007), and sections of John Grasso, *Historical Dictionary of Basketball* (Lanham, MD: Scarecrow Press, 2011) and Frank P. Jozsa Jr. *The National Basketball Association*: *Business*, *Organization and Strategy* (Singapore: World Scientific, 2011).

F.P. Jozsa Jr., *National Basketball Association Strategies*,
SpringerBriefs in Economics 84, DOI 10.1007/978-3-319-10058-6_7

the NBA's traditional orange ball, and had a few regional franchises that played their home games in several cities.

Unlike the NBA, the ABA had flair because its teams' games were not boring but exciting with lots of movement, speed, and fast breaks. Players would run up and down the court, attack the basket 1 min and then shoot three-pointers the next minute. The three-point line, which tended to force defenders to step out and guard respectable outside shooters, opened up the lane for players to dribble the ball and drive to the basket.

The NBA, meanwhile, only had the two-point shot. Thus, teams' defenses tended to huddle close to the basket, encourage outside shots, and not allow much activity to develop near the basket. Furthermore, players did not foul out during ABA games. While NBA stars would sometimes leave a game and sit on the bench for 1 or more minutes due to foul trouble, the ABAs were on the court as much as their bodies and coaches allowed them.

As conceived by former Minneapolis Lakers legend and then ABA Commissioner George Mikan, many players were athletically spectacular, showcased cool moves, wore fashionable clothes, and had a bad attitude but in a good way. Many future NBA stars first played in the ABA. These included, for example, Julius Erving, Moses Malone, Connie Hawkins, Artis Gilmore, George Gervin, and Dan Issel. Besides them, others were Rick Barry, Spencer Haywood, Bobby Jones, Maurice Lucas, Billy Cunningham, and Steve Jones. Some ABA coaches were ambitious, smart, and talented such as Larry Brown, Hubie Brown, K.C. Jones, Lou Carnesecca, Al Bianchi, and Doug Moe.

As a business strategy, the ABA hired four of the best referees in the NBA. In fact, Earl Strom, John Vanak, Norm Drucker, and Joe Gushue each received considerable more money and benefits after joining the ABA. In his memoir *Calling The Shots*, Strom conveys the heady sense of being in demand by a rival league with money to burn and the depression that began the next year when he started refereeing in the ABA and realizing there were many inferior players who performed in obsolete arenas before very small crowds. Nonetheless, the emergence of the new league boosted salaries of these referees and many professional basketball players.[2]

When originally created, ABA teams had less talent than those in the NBA, and in games between the leagues, the NBA dominated them. By the early 1970s, however, the ABA's talent pool increased dramatically in quality. While it is no longer a big deal for current NBA teams to draft high school players after graduation, the league never did that decades ago. Even so, ABA teams drafted high school and college players and therefore attracted young but gifted athletes, who if given the choice, would have been on NBA teams. During the early-to-mid-1970s, ABA teams usually defeated their rivals in interleague competition.

Because the NBA had plenty of money, it advertised and brought fans and much media coverage to the league's games. In comparison, the ABA lacked cash and did not have the assets or resources necessary to draw enough fans and receive the

[2]The book is Earl Strom, *Calling the Shots*: *My Five Decades in the NBA* (New York, NY: Simon & Schuster, 1990).

national attention it deserved. Despite the rise in quality of ABA teams in their regular seasons, the NBA still had fame, fortune, and power while the ABA struggled financially. Although the new league proved itself in many ways–competitively and with exciting games and top-notch basketball stars–it was unable to prove itself and survive as a business.

The freewheeling style of the ABA eventually caught on with fans, but the lack of a national television contract and protracted financial losses would spell doom for the ABA as an independent circuit. During its final year of existence in 1976, the ABA pioneered the now-popular slam-dunk contest at its all-star game in Denver, Colorado.

Table 7.1 lists the ABA teams and their seasons, championships, and histories. Other than four that joined the NBA in 1976, the remaining teams terminated operations

Table 7.1 ABA teams, historical information, 1967–1975 seasons

Team	Seasons	Championships	History
Anaheim Amigos	1	0	Moved to Los Angeles in 1968
Carolina Cougars	5	1	Moved to St. Louis in 1974
Dallas/Texas Chaparrals	6	0	Moved to San Antonio in 1973
Denver Rockets/Nuggets	9	3	Joined NBA in 1976
Houston Mavericks	2	0	Moved to Charlotte in 1969
Indiana Pacers	9	6	Joined NBA in 1976
Kentucky Colonels	9	3	Disbanded in 1976
Los Angeles Stars	3	0	Moved to Salt Lake City in 1970
Memphis Pros/Tams/Sounds	5	0	Disbanded in 1975
Miami Floridians	4	0	Disbanded in 1972
Minnesota Muskies	1	0	Moved to Miami in 1968
Minnesota Pipers	1	0	Moved to Pittsburgh in 1969
New Jersey Americans	1	0	Moved to New York in 1968
New Orleans Buccaneers	3	0	Moved to Memphis in 1970
New York Nets	8	4	Joined NBA in 1976
Oakland Oaks	2	2	Moved to Washington in 1969
Pittsburgh Pipers	1	2	Moved to Minneapolis in 1968
Pittsburgh Pipers/Condors	3	0	Disbanded in 1972
St. Louis Spirits	2	0	Disbanded in 1976
San Antonio Spurs	3	0	Joined NBA in 1976
San Diego Conquistadors/Sails	3	0	Disbanded in 1975
Utah Stars	6	4	Disbanded in 1975
Washington Capitols	1	0	Moved to Norfolk in 1970
Virginia Squires	6	1	Disbanded in 1976

Note: Abbreviations are American Basketball Association (ABA) and National Basketball Association (NBA). The slash (/) indicates change in a team's nickname

Source: James Quirk and Rodney D. Fort, *Pay Dirt: The Business of Professional Team Sports* (Princeton, NJ: Princeton University Press, 1992), 459–63, and "Remember the ABA: Team Histories & Fan Memories" at http://www.remembertheaba.com cited 12 March 2014

and canceled their franchise in years from 1967 to 1976. As such, this section discusses expansion franchises in the ABA and the league's different teams that moved from a city in a metropolitan area to another.

Expansion Franchises

Founded by dentist Dr. Leonard Bloom for $1 million in 1972, the San Diego Conquistadors (nicknamed Q's) were the ABA's first and only expansion team. Because of a personal feud between Bloom and Peter Graham, who managed the city-owned 14,400-seat San Diego Sports Arena, the team did not play its home games in that facility for 2 years. When the conflict between them was resolved in the fall of 1974, it was too late for a weakened franchise that had to play home games for two regular seasons at such bandboxes as 3,200-seat Peterson Gym and multipurpose sports facility, Golden Hall.

After qualifying for the 1973 ABA playoffs in their inaugural season, the Q's seemingly were fortunate by paying center Wilt Chamberlain only $600,000 to become their player-coach. However, the NBA's Los Angeles Lakers successfully sued to block their former star from playing for his new team. Relegated to a sideline role, Chamberlain became an indifferent sideshow who once skipped a game to appear at an autograph session for his recently published autobiography. On that and other occasions, Chamberlain's replacement was Stan Albeck, who later coached the NBA's Chicago Bulls, San Antonio Spurs, and New Jersey Nets. Even so, the Q's were in the postseason again but lost their game in the first round for the second year in a row.

Despite consecutive playoff appearances, the arena situation continued to plague the team. Frustrated with his inability to lease the city's Sports Arena, Bloom announced plans for construction of a 20,000-seat arena in Chula Vista, California. Then a public referendum on the arena, held just after the ABA season started, failed by 294 votes. In hopes of returning to a market abandoned by the Los Angeles Stars 4 years earlier, ABA officials ordered Bloom to take preliminary steps toward moving from San Diego to Los Angeles.

In the 1974–1975 ABA season, the Q's lost Chamberlain but finally obtained a lease to play their home games in the Sports Arena. However, without Chamberlain as a gate attraction, San Diego sports fans ignored the team, which placed last in the Western Division (WD) and missed the 1975 playoffs.

During June 1975, Bloom sold his franchise for $2 million to Frank Goldberg, who was a former co-owner of the successful Denver Nuggets franchise. Goldberg started anew by renaming his team the San Diego Sails for the league's 1975–1976 seasons and then hired former University of Minnesota basketball coach Bill Musselman. With a completely different roster, color scheme, set of uniforms, and about everything else, the Sails sought to repeat the Nuggets' turnaround a season earlier from mediocrity to becoming a championship contender.

In their opening game at home during October 1975, the Sails attracted only 3,060 fans and lost to the Nuggets. After their dismal start of the season, fan attendance rapidly dwindled further as the team had a 3–8 win–loss record. In fact, only 1,670 spectators showed up for the Sail's last home game. Soon thereafter, Goldberg found out his franchise would not be part of the pending ABA–NBA merger. Furthermore, Lakers' owner Jack Kent Cooke supposedly refused to share his team's fan base in southern California with the Sails from San Diego. With his team lacking fan support or a long-term future, Goldberg folded the franchise after they played 11 regular season games in late 1975.

Unlike the increasingly popular NBA, which admitted six new franchises in the 1960s and four in the 1970s, the ABA avoided the operational problems, potential costs, and risks of investing in and expanding into new sports markets. As denoted in Table 7.1, the majority of ABA franchises disbanded after playing a few seasons while 12 moved from sites in cities of metropolitan areas to other urban places.

In addition to these decisions, four ABA clubs joined the NBA in 1976. Simply put, the ABA did not have enough assets, funds and resources, and knowledgeable administrators and executives to commercially, competitively, and realistically challenge the NBA in the long run and thus did not invade different or similar small, midsized, and large basketball markets across America.

Team Relocations

Between 1967 and 1976, a dozen ABA franchises moved their operations to other metropolitan areas. The performances of these teams before and after they relocated are in Table A7.1 of the Appendix. For readers of *National Basketball Association Strategies* to compare, examine, and interpret numbers in the table and population data, next are highlights of this information. Following this section is a brief history of the NBA and then the facts, significance, and consequences of the leagues' merger in 1976.

First, ABA teams that moved from smaller to larger populated areas included the Amigos and Americans in 1968, Pipers in 1969, and Cougars in 1974. Indeed, the cities of Anaheim, Teaneck, and Minneapolis did not have enough enthusiastic basketball fans or local businesses to support their respective club at home more than 1 year while Charlotte hosted the Cougars for five regular seasons before the club moved to St. Louis. Meanwhile, the other eight ABA teams or 66 % of the group relocated to less populated markets such as the Muskies in 1968, Oaks in 1969, Buccaneers in 1970, and Chaparrals in 1973. Apparently, these clubs had better opportunities to survive and succeed at their new rather than former sites.[3]

[3] Table A7.2 contains the populations and population ranks of metropolitan areas that hosted ABA teams before and after they relocated. For some teams, there were significant changes in the size of their home markets. Because they moved to avoid competing for fans with teams in the rival NBA, to reduce their operating costs by moving to smaller cities, and/or simply to enter new sports markets, the ABA's Minnesota Muskies and Houston Mavericks in the 1960s and Los Angeles Stars and Washington Caps in the 1970s, for example, had more opportunities to succeed with new names and nicknames at their post-move sites. Despite being in larger markets, however, other ABA teams failed after a few seasons including the Los Angeles Stars, Pittsburgh Pipers/Condors, and St. Louis Spirits.

Second, 9 or 75 % of the ABA teams in Table A7.1 played more seasons after relocating to sites in other metropolitan areas. For example, the Nets and Squires had, respectively, seven and five additional seasons in New York City and Norfolk while the Capitols, Spurs, and Spirits franchises were able to exist longer before moving from Oakland, Dallas, and Charlotte. Interestingly, the Pipers played one season each in Pittsburgh and the Minneapolis area before moving again in 1969. As a group, the teams doubled their number of seasons from their pre-move to post-move sites.

Third, ABA teams were in 18 playoffs before and 31 after relocating to other metropolitan areas. Among them, the most successful in number of playoff appearances included the Nets, Stars, and Squires while the Spurs and Spirits had fewer opportunities to participate in playoffs at their new homes, in part, because of fewer seasons. In contrast to them, the Pipers/Cougars existed more seasons in Pittsburgh than did the Pipers in Minneapolis yet failed to win enough games to appear in any playoffs.

Fourth, the Nets from 1968 and Stars from 1970 each won four more championships at their post-move than pre-move sites. Most likely, they had talented players and experienced coaches for several seasons while those on other teams decided to sign contracts and perform or coach elsewhere after 1 or 2 years. Thus, the two former teams dominated their opponents in division and championship series.

Fifth, the criteria in Table A7.1 denotes that the most successful relocations were the New Jersey Americans to New York in 1968 and 2 years later, Los Angeles Stars to Utah and Washington Capitols to Virginia. Alternatively, the least successful moves were the Pittsburgh Pipers to Minneapolis in 1968, Oakland Oaks to Washington in 1969, and Carolina Cougars to St. Louis in 1974. Besides them, the Dallas Chaparrals to San Antonio in 1974 was an important relocation because in 1976 the Spurs joined the NBA.

National Basketball Association

The BAA and NBL merger in 1949 created the NBA. The new league, which had 17 franchises located in a mix of small, midsized, and large cities, had teams playing their games in big arenas and tiny armories and gymnasiums. In 1950, the NBA consolidated to 11 franchises, a process that continued until the 1953–1954 regular season when it totaled 8 franchises, all of which are current members of the league.

During the 1950s, contraction caused the NBA's small-city franchises to move to larger cities such as the Hawks from the Tri-Cities to Milwaukee in 1951 and Pistons from Fort Wayne, Indiana to Detroit, Michigan in 1957. The first African-American player, Harold Hunter, signed with the Washington Capitols in 1950 but then cut from the team during training camp. Later, other blacks played on teams including the Capitols' Earl Lloyd, Celtics' Chuck Cooper, and Knicks' Nathaniel "Sweetwater" Clifton.

Led by center George Mikan, the Minneapolis Lakers won five championships and became the NBA's first dynasty team. To encourage shooting and discourage stalling, the league introduced the 24-s shot clock in 1954. If a team did not attempt to score a field goal or the ball failed to make contact with the rim within 24 s of obtaining the ball, play stopped and the ball given to the opponent.

In 1957 rookie center Bill Russell joined the NBA Celtics, who already featured guard Bob Cousy and coach Red Auerbach, and led the club to 11 championships in 13 seasons. Center Wilt Chamberlain entered the league with the Philadelphia Warriors in 1959 and became a dominant individual star of the 1960s, setting new single game records in scoring and rebounding. Indeed, Russell's rivalry with Chamberlain became one of the greatest in the history of American team sports.

Through the 1960s, the NBA continued to strengthen geographically with the shift of various teams to Los Angeles, San Francisco, Philadelphia and Atlanta, and the addition of its first expansion franchises. During 1966–1968, the league expanded from 9 to 14 teams that had home sites in Chicago, Seattle, San Diego, Milwaukee, and Phoenix.

In 1967, the league faced a new external threat with the formation of the ABA. These leagues engaged in a bidding war with the NBA landing the most important college star of the era, Lew Alcindor (renamed Kareem Abdul-Jabbar). However, the NBA's leading scorer jumped to the ABA and so did four veteran referees.

In 1969, designer Alan Siegel created the modern NBA logo. It had a silhouette of the legendary player Jerry West based on a photo by Wen Roberts, although NBA officials denied a particular player influenced it because, according to Siegel, "They want to institutionalize it rather than individualize it. It's become such an ubiquitous, classic symbol and focal point of their identity and their licensing program that they don't necessarily want to identify it with one player." The iconic logo debuted in 1971 and remains a fixture of the NBA brand.[4]

ABA teams succeeded in attracting a number of major basketball stars in the late 1960s to early 1970s, in part, because they were able to sign college undergraduates. Meanwhile, the NBA expanded rapidly during this period, one purpose being to play their games in the sports' most viable cities. From 1966 to 1974, the NBA grew from 9 to 18 franchises.

In 1970, the Portland Trail Blazers, Cleveland Cavaliers, and Buffalo Braves (now Los Angeles Clippers) made their debuts expanding the league to 17 teams. The New Orleans Jazz (now Utah Jazz) joined the NBA in 1974 bringing the total to 18 clubs. Following the 1976 postseason, the leagues reached a settlement that provided for the admission of four ABA franchises into the NBA, raising the number of franchises to 22.

ABA–NBA Merger

Three years after the new league opened its first season, NBA owners voted 13–4 to pursue a merger with the ABA. Seattle Supersonics owner Sam Schulman, who was a member of the merger committee in 1970, was so eager to consolidate the leagues

[4] See "The Story of the NBA Logo" at http://www.logodesignlove.com cited 19 March 2014.

that he publicly said if the NBA did not accept the agreement, he would transfer the Supersonics from the NBA to ABA. In addition, the ABA Dallas Chaparrals owners were so confident of the impending merger that they suggested the ABA delay scheduling and playing a regular season and postseason in 1971–1972. Thus, most team owners and the leagues' two commissioners supported the merger during the early 1970s.

Before the 1971–1972 basketball season, the ABA and NBA met in an interleague all-star game, which the NBA won 125–120. In the same preseason, ABA and NBA teams began to compete against each other in exhibition games. At the first exhibition played in September 1971, the NBA's Milwaukee Bucks narrowly defeated the Dallas Chaparrals. Gradually, the ABA began to prove its superiority in games by winning 15–10 against the NBA in 1973, 16–7 in 1974, and 31–17 in 1975. Overall, the ABA won more of these interleague games than did the NBA, and in every matchup of reigning champions from the two leagues, the ABA champion won including the final premerger season when the Kentucky Colonels beat the Golden State Warriors.

Early attempts at merging the ABA and NBA were in suspense for years because of litigation known as the Oscar Robertson suit. After NBA owners voted in 1970 to merge with the ABA, the NBA Players Association filed a lawsuit in April 1970 to prevent the merger on antitrust grounds. The existence of the ABA resulted in increased salaries for players in both leagues as the ABA and NBA competed with each other to sign players. Although finally settled in February 1976, the Oscar Robertson suit presented an insurmountable obstacle to the eventual merger of the two leagues.

During early-to-mid-1972, Congress was close to enacting legislation to enable a merger between the leagues despite the Oscar Robertson suit. Then in late September, a US Senate committee had reportedly adopted a specific merger bill. However, the bill was put together to benefit franchise owners and ended up not pleasing enough Senators or the teams' players. Subsequently, the bill failed without coming to a floor vote. When Congress reconvened in 1973, the Senate reviewed another merger bill but did not process it any further.

Because of the legislation's failure, the ABA installed a new commissioner, Mike Storen, whose focus was the future merger of the two leagues as equals. Alex Hannum, who had coached teams in both the NBA and ABA, said about Storen, "The most important problem he has is still the merger with the NBA. And, I believe his approach is just right for us. Storen wants to build our league to be the strongest. Then he can negotiate with the NBA as an equal."[5]

---

[5] In a statement to the media, *Sports Illustrated* noted "the tactics Storen says the ABA will employ sound a good deal more like those used by American Football League Commissioner Al Davis in the last days of the football war than a plan for peaceful coexistence. The ABA has reinstituted its $300 million antitrust suit against the NBA. It also may move some franchises into better TV [television] markets, an ill-advised maneuver that will mean going against established NBA teams on their home turf. And for the first time since 1970, the ABA will go after established NBA players. We will have exploratory contract talks with lots of their men" said Storen. "Whether we'll sign none, six or ten of them will depend on how things work out. But you can be sure of one thing: we'll do this in a serious, orderly way." See Peter Carry, "Having a Ball With the ABA" at http://www.sportsillustrated.com cited 18 March 2014.

Before basketball's 1975–1976 season, the ABA's Denver Nuggets and New York Nets each applied to join the NBA. In fact, owners of these teams had approached owner John Y. Brown Jr. in an attempt to get his Kentucky Colonels to join their attempted leap to the NBA, but Brown refused, saying he was loyal to the ABA. Ultimately, a court order forced the Nuggets and Nets to play a lame-duck season in the ABA. Anyway, the Nuggets and Nets' attempted move into the NBA created a great deal of ill will within the ABA, and brought attention to the emerging financial weakness of some of the league's weakest teams.

Meanwhile, the ABA had three of its teams disband near the end of 1975. Before the Memphis Sounds moved to Maryland permanently and become the Baltimore Claws, the club folded after only three preseason games when it failed to post a performance bond with the league. Then in November 1975, or 3 weeks into the regular season, the San Diego Sails folded. The Sails had been plagued by small attendances at their home games and owner Frank Goldberg learned the team would most likely be excluded from any upcoming ABA–NBA merger because Los Angeles Lakers' owner Jack Kent Cooke did not want competition in Southern California for either his team or their coverage on the cable television system he owned. Subsequently, the Sails' players entered a special dispersal draft.

Shortly afterward, one of the league's longstanding and successful teams, Utah Stars, folded during December 1975 because of not meeting its payroll. One year earlier, Stars' owner Bill Daniels went bankrupt due to his unsuccessful campaign to become Governor of Colorado and his financial difficulties with other business ventures. Eventually, Daniels paid back the Stars' season ticket holders in full plus 8 % interest. There were discussions between the Stars and St. Louis Spirits about merging their operations. Nonetheless, the Stars folded before anything happened between them. Including superstar Moses Malone, the Stars sold most of their players to the Spirits. With the ABA reduced to seven teams, the league abandoned divisional play.

Another popular, respected, and formerly powerful ABA team, the Virginia Squires, struggled competitively in their final 2 years. Blessed with remarkable talent in previous seasons, the Squires sold such fan favorites as Julius Erving, Rick Barry, George Gervin, and Swen Nater because of constant financial problems. In the ABA's 1974–1975 season, the once-successful Squires posted a league-worst record of 15–69. Then in their next regular season, the Squires tied their own mark by posting the identical win–loss record. Moreover, due to dwindling attendances at their home games, the Squires fought to survive until the end of the season. Indeed, on several occasions, the Squires were barely able to pay their players. By the end of the 1975–1976 season, the Squires were completely out of money. Although it was apparent even before then that they would not be part of a merger, the ABA folded them during May 1976 after the franchise failed to pay a $75,000 assessment to the league.

After the Squires terminated operations, the Kentucky Colonels, led by center Artis Gilmore, defeated the Indiana Pacers in the first round of the 1976 ABA playoffs. The Colonels, in turn, lost a seven-game semifinal series to the Denver Nuggets, led by Dan Issel and David Thompson. Later, the Nuggets lost the ABA Finals to the New York Nets who had defeated the San Antonio Spurs to get there. The St. Louis Spirits, meanwhile, survived the regular season but missed the playoffs.

With the Oscar Robertson suit settled, these six teams were still operating when the ABA and NBA commenced their final merger negotiations. On June 17, 1976, the leagues merged at the NBA meetings in the Cape Cod Room at Dunfey's Hyannis Resort in Hyannis, Massachusetts. As a result, the Nets, Nuggets, Pacers, and Spurs became franchises in the NBA while the Colonels and Squires went out of business but received $2.8 million each as compensation from the other four ABA teams.[6]

Due to the merger, the NBA imposed the following terms on the four ABA refugees: First, the new teams' arrival expanded the senior league and each of them had to pay a $3.2 million fee to the NBA by September 15, 1976. Second, the New York Nets had to pay an additional $4.8 million directly to their in-town rival, the New York Knicks, as compensation for invading the New York metropolitan area.

Third, the four former ABA teams would not receive any television money during their first three seasons in the NBA and had to pay one-seventh of their annual television revenues after that to the owners of the defunct St. Louis Spirits in perpetuity. Fourth, these new NBA teams would receive no votes related to the distribution of gate receipts or the alignment of NBA divisions for 2 years. Fifth, the remaining players from the Kentucky Colonels and St. Louis Spirits were available to NBA teams through a dispersal draft, with superstars such as Artis Gilmore and Moses Malone joining teams other than the four from the ABA.

In short, the indemnities and other penalties imposed on the four ABA franchises were as draconian as the penalties that the American Football League teams faced when they joined the National Football League (NFL) in 1970. In addition to those payments and restrictions, the NBA would not recognize any ABA records.

To highlight their contributions as competitors and business enterprises, the following is an overview of the four former ABA teams and their performances while playing in divisions and conferences of the NBA.[7]

Denver Nuggets

From 1976 to 2013, the Nuggets had periods of success. While appearing in 24 playoffs including 9 consecutive seasons in the 1980s, the team won 7 division titles but zero conference championships. Historically, the Nuggets' most productive head coaches were Doug Moe during the 1980s and George Karl in the 2000s. After playing their home games in the 17,000-seat McNichols Sports Arena through

[6] Other readings about the ABA–NBA merger include Curry Kirkpatrick, "A Season For All Men," *Sports Illustrated* (25 October 1976), 34; "Basketball," *Sports Illustrated* (17 February 1977), 116; Frank DeFord, "One Last Hurrah in Hyannis," *Sports Illustrated* (28 June 1976), 64; Bill Rhoden, "ABA Superstars Join the NBA," *Ebony* (January 1977), 88–89.

[7] Recent financial data about NBA franchises was in Kurt Badenhausen, Mike Ozanian, and Christina Settimi, "NBA Team Values: The Business of Basketball" at http://www.forbes.com cited 6 February 2014. For teams' historical attendances, players, and coaches, see "Rodney D. Fort's Sports Business Data" at http://sites.google.com cited 5 February 2014, the *Official NBA Guide: 2013–14 Edition* (New York, NY: NBA Properties, 2013), and the *Official NBA Register: 2013–14 Edition* (New York, NY: NBA Properties, 2013).

the NBA's 1998–1999 season, the Nuggets now share the 19,155-seat Pepsi Center with the National Hockey League (NHL) Colorado Avalanche.

Although the Nuggets finished their 2012–2013 season with a franchise record of 57 wins, they lost in the first round of the WC playoffs to the Golden State Warriors. George Karl was the NBA Coach of the Year but then fired after overseeing eight first round playoff exits in 9 years. The club also let General Manager Masai Ujiri leave for the same job with the Toronto Raptors after he won an Executive of the Year award.

Team owner Stan Kroenke, who besides the Avalanche also owns the NFL St. Louis Rams, Major League Soccer Colorado Rapids, and Arsenal of the English Premier League, increased his sports empire in March 2013 by acquiring the Outdoor Channel. Among franchise organizations, the Nuggets are an above-average team that needs to win an NBA championship to become more popular with sports fans in the Denver market.

Indiana Pacers

Since established in 1967, the Pacers have been successful especially by winning three ABA championships. While in the NBA for 38 seasons, the team qualified for 21 playoffs and won five division titles besides a conference title in 2000. Such great athletes as Reggie Miller, Chris Mullin, Alex English, Mel Daniels, and Roger Brown played in regular seasons and some postseasons for the Pacers. In addition, the team's former coaches include Larry Bird, Bob Hill, and Larry Brown during the 1990s and in the 2000s, former Indiana University All-American Isiah Thomas, Rick Carlisle, and Jim O'Brien.

Hometown fans are finally embracing the Pacers after seven straight seasons of ranking twenty-fifth or worse in attendance. Before the 2013–2014 NBA season, the team's individual ticket sales were up 50 % and package sales 30 % while 18,165-seat Bankers Life Fieldhouse was at 93 % of capacity in games halfway through a recent season. The Pacers became the first franchise to sell on-court advertising in October 2013 when it endorsed a 2-year deal with the Indiana Economic Development Corporation. Actually, after the league relaxed its rules about on-court advertisements, it was the first team to take advantage of that change.

New Jersey/Brooklyn Nets

Between 1976 and 2013, the Nets appeared in 16 playoffs and won four division and two conference titles. During various seasons, the team's key players included guards Jason Kidd and Vince Carter, and forwards Buck Williams and Derrick Coleman. Such coaches as Larry Brown and Stan Albeck in the 1980s, Chuck Daly and Butch Beard in the 1990s, and Lawrence Frank and Byron Scott in the 2000s led the Nets in their division of the EC.

Regarding news since relocating from New Jersey in 2012, the Nets' billionaire owner Mikhail Prokhorov has been generous and not spared any expense to bring an NBA title to Brooklyn. Before the 2013–2014 NBA season, he signed off on a player payroll of $101 million, which carried a luxury tax bill of several million dollars.

From playing their home games at the new $1 billion, 18,103-seat Barclays Center, the Nets will increase their gate receipts, revenue, operating income, and estimated market value as a sports enterprise. This, in turn, should make the team more entertaining and competitive in the EC's Atlantic Division and eventually enough to challenge for a conference title and league championship.

San Antonio Spurs

According to opinions of sports experts, this is the most efficient, successful, and well-organized NBA franchise. Since 1976, the team has been in 35 playoffs including 2000–2014, and won 20 division and 6 conference titles, and 5 league championships. Retired but outstanding Spurs' players were forwards George Gervin and Bruce Bowen, and centers Artis Gilmore and David Robinson. In the 2000s, forward Tim Duncan and guards Tony Parker and Manu Ginobilli have been the team's most valuable players. For years, they and Coach Gregg Popovich have been leaders of Spurs' teams.

This franchise has the highest winning percentage in major professional sports and won at least 60 % of its game in any season since drafting Tim Duncan in 1997. Sixteen years later, the Spurs were within seconds of adding a fifth ring before eventually falling to the Miami Heat in seven games during the NBA Finals. Then in June 2014, the club won its fifth league championship defeating the Heat in five games.

The team's playoff series and a payroll below the luxury tax helped boost operating profits to a record $39 million. Profits could have been even greater, but the Spurs swept two of their playoff foes, which limited the number of home games played at the 18,588-seat AT&T Center in San Antonio. Although ratings for Spurs games on Fox Sports Southwest were down more than 35 % in their 2012–2013 regular season, they were third highest in the NBA.[8]

[8] For additional sources about the short- and long-run effects of the ABA–NBA merger in 1976, read such books as Peter C. Bjarkman, *The Encyclopedia of Pro Basketball Team Histories* (New York, NY: Carroll & Graf, 1994); Connie Kirchberg, *Hoop Love: A History of the National Basketball Association* (Jefferson, NC: McFarland, 2007); James Quirk and Rodney D. Fort, Pay Dirt: The Business of Professional Team Sports (Princeton, NJ: Princeton University Press, 1992); Leonard Koppett, *Total Basketball: The Ultimate Basketball Encyclopedia* (Wilmington, DE: Sport Classic Books, 2004); Jan Hubbard, *The Official NBA Encyclopedia* (New York, NY: Doubleday, 2000). Information about various teams is available online in readings at various websites. See, for example, "Basketball History" at http://www.history-of-basketball.com cited 20 September 2005; "History of Basketball" at http://library.thinkquest.org cited 24 August 2009; "National Basketball Association (NBA) History" at http://www.rauzulusstreet.com cited 12 August 2005; "NBA Growth Timetable" at http://www.basketball.com cited 17 September 2005; "Professional Basketball Leagues" at http://apbr.org cited 22 August 2009.

Chapter 8
Future Strategies

Expansion Franchises

Since 1949, several new franchises had their team playing in one or more regular seasons and postseasons of the National Basketball Association (NBA). Six of them joined the league in the 1960s, four in the 1970s, five in the 1980s, two in the 1990s, and one in the 2000s. Among the group, 11 are at home at their original sites while the other seven moved from cities in metropolitan areas to different locations. Regarding the former teams, the least and most recent of them ranged, respectively, from the Chicago Bulls in 1966 to Charlotte Bobcats in 2004, and for those that relocated, they extended in years from the Chicago Zephyrs to Baltimore, Maryland in 1963 to Vancouver Grizzlies to Memphis, Tennessee in 2001.

If NBA officials decide for demographic, economic, sport-specific, and other reasons to increase the size of their league after 2014, some cities in the United States (US) and foreign countries with at least an appropriate-sized public or private sports arena might welcome, host, and support a new professional basketball team. In other words, a syndicate of investors who represent city X, metropolitan area Y, and/or region Z would bid for an NBA expansion franchise and if successful, then locate and operate it there. The following are current but unoccupied US and foreign basketball markets and their qualifications to host a new NBA team (Table 8.1).

Domestic Markets

Kansas City

This is a midsized American city without a professional basketball franchise. Although it is not near any existing NBA teams–the closest are in Oklahoma City, Chicago, Memphis, and Denver–the new Sprint Center has hosted Big 12 and

F.P. Jozsa Jr., *National Basketball Association Strategies*,
SpringerBriefs in Economics 84, DOI 10.1007/978-3-319-10058-6_8

Table 8.1 Potential NBA expansion markets, Post-2014

Domestic site	Population	Arena	Foreign site	Population	Arena
Kansas City	464,310	Sprint Center	Barcelona	1,620,943	Palau Sant Jordi
Las Vegas	596,424	New Las Vegas Arena	Berlin	3,462,410	O2 World Berlin
Louisville	605,110	KFC Yum Center	London	9,005,300	O2 Arena
Pittsburgh	306,211	Consol Energy Center	Madrid	6,574,450	Palacio de DePortes
Seattle	634,535	Key Arena	Paris	10,620,100	Palais Omnisports
St. Louis	318,172	Scottrade Center	Rome	3,298,300	PalaLottomatica

Note: Population is for each city in hundreds of thousands. See Table A8.1 for the population of US cities' metropolitan areas in 2012
Source: *World Almanac and Book of Facts* (New York, NY: Simon & Schuster, 2014)

National Collegiate Athletic Association (NCAA) basketball tournament games and other events. Kansas City is in a metropolitan area of the Midwest that cares about basketball, had more Final Fours than anywhere else, home to the College Basketball Hall of Fame, and less than an hour away from Lawrence, Kansas. The City's only drawback is competition for sports fans from such professional teams in the area as the National Football League (NFL) Kansas City Chiefs and Major League Baseball (MLB) Kansas City Royals, and from such college basketball teams as the University of Kansas Jayhawks and Kansas State Wildcats.

Las Vegas

Whenever people mention NBA expansion, someone points out that Las Vegas is the biggest US city without major professional sports. While it is the only non-NBA site to host the league's all-star game, the Utah Jazz has played home games there. The Sacramento Kings considered moving to and operating at home in Las Vegas, but there were too many problems. Still, the city is not that large of a sports market and has been stagnant in growth from the housing foreclosure crisis during and after 2008. Most likely, Las Vegas would build a new arena and fill it for home NBA games. Even so, sports betting scandals there will probably keep the NBA out of Nevada.

Louisville

A potential market for an expansion NBA team, Louisville has a new arena. It is the 22,000-seat KFC Yum Center, which is located downtown and has the perfect name for a reincarnation of the former American Basketball Association (ABA) Kentucky Colonels. The state is a college basketball market with major sports program at the University of Louisville and another one in Lexington for the University of Kentucky

Wildcats. CBS Sports once reported that Louisville was a possible Sacramento Kings landing site, although that did not have the credibility of a Kings movement to Anaheim, Las Vegas, or San Jose.

There are at least two problems with Louisville as a future home of an NBA team. One is that the city's metropolitan area is relatively small to host a professional basketball team in the long term. Indeed, most one-team markets of NBA, NFL, and National Hockey League (NHL) teams in American towns do not prosper for decades. In fact, some of the NBA's current but small-market clubs deplete their cash and complain to be at a competitive disadvantage. Besides market size, proximity to other NBA teams is also a problem for the city. Although none of them exist in Cincinnati or Nashville, which is different than in the NFL, nearby are the Indianapolis Pacers. That, in turn, may be legally troublesome if the NBA approves an expansion team in Louisville.

Pittsburgh

Similar to Kansas City, Pittsburgh has a shiny new 19,100-seat arena named the Consol Energy Center. For a few months, there were rumors that the Detroit Pistons were moving to Pittsburgh, which was a city mentioned by the former NBA Commissioner David Stern as a possible relocation site. Indeed, Pittsburgh has some of the most dedicated, loyal, and sincere sports fans in the nation and basketball tradition at Pittsburgh and Duquesne Universities. If the NBA wants to put another team in the Northeast or Eastern Midwest, Pittsburgh seems like the best choice. A drawback is the size of the Pittsburgh area, which has been in decline and among the smallest of markets of teams in MLB and the NFL and NHL. Nevertheless, in an era when a one-team market does not seem feasible, a fourth professional sports club in western Pennsylvania may be appropriate for the NBA.

Seattle

Of any domestic city in Table 8.1, Seattle has plenty of sports fans who demand an NBA team and furthermore, it is the largest American market area without one. However, if Seattle wants a second incarnation of the Supersonics, the new team's ownership group will realize that 17,000-seat Key Arena needs renovation or replacement with a larger, lucrative, and more modern facility.

Although upgraded 16 years ago and the home site of the Women's National Basketball Association (WNBA) Seattle Storm and Seattle University–who each play there without any problems–a prospective franchise owner such as Clayton Bennett wants improvements to the venue since it is too small to meet NBA standards. Another question, will the Pacific Northwest support two professional basketball teams again? Most likely, yes, although there are more people in the Los Angeles metropolitan area than the Northwest and hundreds of empty seats exist at Los Angeles Clippers games.

St. Louis

In the Midwest, this is a traditional basketball city and besides Seattle and San Diego, the third largest metropolitan area without an NBA team. While Kansas City is the traditional seat of Big Eight college basketball, so is St. Louis with the Missouri Valley Conference. Both the 22,000-seat Scottrade Center, which is the most likely site and the 66,000-seat Edward Jones Dome have hosted NCAA tournament games. However, St. Louis faces other problems than Kansas City. Indeed, it has the dubious distinction of hosting three defunct professional basketball franchises–two former NBA and one ABA team–that it shares with Baltimore and San Diego. While Scottrade arena and the Dome are at least 16-years-old, St. Louis is close to existing markets in Chicago, Indianapolis, and Memphis. It seems likely, however, that St. Louis would not get an NBA expansion team if another one were currently in Kansas City.[1]

Foreign Markets

Barcelona

This is the second largest city and metropolitan area in Spain and sixth most populated urban area in the European Union. Barcelona hosted many major international tournaments before 2014 and is home to professional teams in different sports. Opened in 1990, the city's 17,000-seat Palau Sant Jordi was the site of the 1998, 2003, and 2011 Euroleague final four basketball series, 1997 and 2012 EuroBasket semifinals and finals, 2012 Spanish Basketball Cup, and one of six sites of the 2014 International Basketball Federation (FIBA) World Cup. Meanwhile, FC Barcelona has won 17 championships in Spain's ACB professional basketball league through 2013, and since 1990, NBA teams have played and won three or 42 % of their games with FC Barcelona at the Palau Sant Jordi.

[1] In the Appendix, Table A8.1 contains the populations and population ranks of ten potential sites for NBA teams. To compare them, San Diego and Seattle, respectively, are the most populated cities and metropolitan areas while Pittsburgh and Louisville, respectively, are the least populated cities and metropolitan areas. For those with a metropolitan area population greater than two million, the likely sites for a new NBA team are Seattle and St. Louis assuming these cities have a new or renovated arena. For sites with a population less than two million, the most attractive of them are Nashville and then Jacksonville and Louisville. Based on factors besides population, the least attractive sites are Baltimore, Kansas City, and Las Vegas. That is because former NBA teams failed in Baltimore and Kansas City, and gambling is legal in Las Vegas. Other than the US, the league may expand and locate a new team in a large foreign city such as Berlin, London, or Madrid.

Berlin

The 2011 NBA champion Dallas Mavericks, led by German-born superstar Dirk Nowitzki, played the Alba Berlin team in Germany's 14,500-seat O2 World Berlin during October 2012. The game, which took place within the NBA Europe Live Tour, was the first for Nowitzki and the Mavericks in Germany. It was the second time, however, that a game with an NBA team occurred at the arena. In 2008, the Washington Wizards played the New Orleans Hornets in Germany's capital city.

Alba Berlin, the anchor tenant at O2 World Berlin and the most successful German basketball club since the late 1990s, has eight championships and six wins in the German Cup. Besides NBA games, the arena hosted the 2008–2009 Euroleague final four basketball series.

London

In January 2013, the NBA returned to London with its third regular season game in Europe. That event included the three-time champion Detroit Pistons and two-time champion New York Knicks. Since 2007, the city's O2 Arena has hosted seven NBA games including four preseason games. Opened in 2007, the 20,000-seat O2 Arena contained the 2012 Summer Olympics and the 2013 Euroleague final four series. In fact, it is the world's busiest venue for concerts and shows with more than two million ticket sales per year.

"London was the epicenter of global sports this summer [2012], and the Olympics were a tremendous showcase for basketball," said the former NBA Commissioner David Stern. "Playing our third regular season game in the city in 3 years and having historic franchises like the Knicks and Pistons serve as our ambassadors provide extraordinary opportunities to further the game's growth and development in the UK and throughout Europe."[2]

Madrid

Opened in 1960 but rebuilt as of 2005, the 15,000-seat Palacio de Deportes is home to Spain's Real Madrid Baloncesto professional basketball team. During the 2000s, the arena hosted such events as the knockout stage of the 2007 Eurobasket, 2008 Euroleague final four, final stages of the 2006, 2009, and 2011 Copa del Rey basketball tournament, and finals of the 2014 FIBA Basketball World Cup.

Founded in 1931, Real Madrid Baloncesto is a division of the Real Madrid club and plays in Spain's ACB League and internationally in the Euroleague. The most successful of its peers in the nation and across Europe, the team has records including 31 League championships, 24 Spanish Cup championships, 8 Euroleague

---

[2] See "NBA Returning to London For Regular Season Matchup" at http://www.nba.com cited 21 March 2014.

championships, and four Saporta Cups. Thus, an NBA expansion team has an opportunity to succeed in Madrid because of the city's large fan base, experience with professional basketball, and its sports culture.

Paris

According to the NBA's business plan, there are more fans watching basketball games on television and players' jerseys being sold at retail outlets in China and Europe than at businesses in North America. A few years ago, NBA officials including former Commissioner David Stern discussed playing the league's all-star game in Paris, France and eventually establishing a European Division with current but struggling small-market teams and new franchises in Eastern and Western Europe.

Although London's O2 Arena has a larger capacity than does France's 14,000-seat Palais Omnisports, Paris is a candidate for an NBA expansion franchise because it hosted the 1999 European Basketball Championship and 2010 Euroleague final four and recommended as a site for an all-star game. Moreover, France is more of a basketball-playing nation than Great Britain. Consequently, if the NBA's future European Division consists only of regional clubs, then Paris sports fans would likely support a team from their hometown.

Rome

A founding member of FIBA, Italy has one of the longest and most consistent basketball traditions in the world. Historically, the country won two gold medals, four silver medals, and four bronze medals at the FIBA EuroBasket tournament, two silver medals at the Summer Olympic Games, and participated in 34 Eurobasket events, 8 World Cups, and 11 Summer Olympic Games. The Basket League A Series is the first-tier level club competition in Italian professional basketball, which determines the national champion.

Opened in 1960 and then renovated in 2003, the 11,200-seat PalaLottomatica hosted the 1960 Olympic basketball tournament, 1991 European basketball championship, and 1997 Euroleague final four series. Currently, it is the home arena of Italy's prestigious Lottomatica Roma professional basketball team.

Anybody who has seen how difficult it has been for an expansion team like Charlotte to get competitive might flinch at the thought, but Mavericks' owner Mark Cuban said that expansion in the NBA probably is on the horizon. "There's a good chance of it happening, but I have no idea when." He said the key to getting a thirty-first NBA franchise, or perhaps two at a time, will be the fee those cities/owners are willing to pay to enter the league. "I just think the price of the expansion fee has to be so high that the NBA owners think, "OK, we're crazy not to do it. What that number is, I don't know. But I'm open to it. It just depends on the price. If it's the price of the last one, no. I thought that was a huge mistake and I voted against it. It just depends on the price."

When the Charlotte Bobcats entered the league in 2004–2005, the expansion fee was $300 million. "When you sit in the board of governors' meeting, you give a price and each NBA owner calculates his share. You balance it to what you're giving up in

TV and shared revenue, and you say OK, it's worth it. Then you say you got to do it." Cuban is a firm believer that another expansion will happen before the league relocates a current franchise. "We talk to them all the time about it. Whenever it comes our turn again, we'll take it. It's hard to top what we did last time, including the snow."[3]

Team Relocations

For demographic, economic, and/or sport-specific reasons, several NBA teams moved from their home sites in small, midsized, and large cities of US metropolitan areas, and from one in Canada, to other urban places. More specifically, four of them changed their locations in the 1950s, five in the 1960s, seven in the 1970s, two in the 1980s, and four in the 2000s. Historically, the first and last moves were, respectively, the Tri-Cities Blackhawks to Milwaukee in 1951 and 61 years later, the New Jersey Nets to Brooklyn, New York.

Regarding their status at their post-move sites, 8 or 36 % of the group had to relocate while the others performed during NBA pre-seasons, regular seasons, and postseasons, and thus are current teams in the league. As of 2013, the oldest and most recent clubs at their current sites are, respectively, the 57-year-old Detroit Pistons and 2-year-old Brooklyn Nets.

Because of their arena contract, community support, financial status, and historical performances in NBA regular seasons and postseasons, such Eastern Conference (EC) teams as the Atlantic Division (AD) Boston Celtics, Brooklyn Nets, and New York Knicks, Central Division (CD) Chicago Bulls, Detroit Pistons, and Indiana Pacers, and Southeast Division (SED) Atlanta Hawks, Miami Heat, and Washington Wizards are least likely to move from their current sites after 2014. Similarly, in the Western Conference (WC), these teams are the Northwest Division (NWD) Denver Nuggets, Oklahoma City Thunder, and Portland Trail Blazers, Pacific Division (PD) Golden State Warriors, Los Angeles Lakers, and Phoenix Suns, and Southwest Division (SWD) Dallas Mavericks, Houston Rockets, and San Antonio Spurs. In other words, most NBA teams will remain at their current homes in cities for more years if not decades.[4]

---

[3] Eddie Sefko, "Mark Cuban: NBA expansion Will Happen Before Relocation, If the Price is Right" at http://www.mavsblogdallasnews.com cited 14 April 2014.

[4] The NBA Kings and city of Sacramento have been working for more than a decade to replace the aging Sleep Train Arena, which opened in 1988 and located outside downtown. The team's new 18,500-seat arena, which cost about $448 million to build with a $190 million contribution from the Kings, will be downtown on the site of an old mall. Finalizing the arena project with new Kings Owner Vivek Ranadive was central to the deal to keep the team in Sacramento after a Seattle-based group made a strong bid to buy and relocate the franchise in 2014–2015. Ranadive's group formally purchased the land for the arena, known as the Downtown Plaza, for an undisclosed sum. Construction will begin in the summer of 2014. New York based Turner Construction, which is general contractor for the arena, is popular in the Sacramento area having built the new Terminal B at Sacramento International Airport and other projects on time and under budget. Regarding details about the arena and other aspects of the project, there are articles in the Sacramento Bee online at http://www.sacbee.com.

Although the league is constructive, determined, and open-minded to evaluate and approve or reject movements of any teams, some of them have various problems and therefore, for one reason or another, are vulnerable and not stable or truly permanent at their current sites. By conference, the following NBA franchises are most likely to move within 10 years from their home sites to another city in a metropolitan area.[5]

Eastern Conference

Atlanta Hawks

Although the Atlanta Hawks appeared in consecutive EC playoffs during the 2008–2012 NBA seasons, the club ranked 21st in league attendance averaging 15.8 thousand per game at the 18,200-seat Philips Arena and placed among the bottom ten teams. They won 58 % of their games, which apparently meant nothing to an unenthusiastic fan base. With poor ticket sales but having such marketable players as Al Horford and Josh Smith, both in their mid-20s, the Hawks are a prime candidate to pursue a move from Atlanta.

In 2013, the team was worth $425 million, which ranked 27th in the NBA, and had a debt-to-value ratio of 55 % and an operating income of –$3.6 million. Although owners Bruce Levenson and Michael Gearon invested millions in their Georgia franchise, it would be hard for them to pass up on an opportunity to move the Hawks from Atlanta to another city.

With high-profile names, a pedigree of success, and an unsupportive fan base, the Hawks are the perfect franchise to leave their home site assuming its front office approves and then agrees to find a buyer of the organization. Although the Hawks were for sale in the summer of 2013, the deal to sell them would come with an expensive arena lease making it difficult to relocate any time soon. In addition, the club has a $75 million early termination penalty with the city.

Charlotte Bobcats

From the 2008–2009 to 2012–2013 NBA seasons, the Bobcats were in two playoffs but won only 34 % of their regular season games. Moreover, their attendances at the 19,000-seat Time Warner Cable Arena ranked 25th in the league at 15.2 thousand

[5]For more information, see Bob Condotta, "Which Struggling NBA Teams Could be Next on Seattle's Target List?" at http://www.seattletimes.com cited 22 March 2014; Maxwell Ogden, "5 NBA Teams Most Likely to Relocate to Seattle Before David Stern Retires" at http://www.bleacherre-port. com cited 22 March 2014; Ted Leroux, "Milwaukee Bucks Destined to Relocate to Seattle or Las Vegas" at http://www.bleacherreport.com cited 23 March 2014.

per game. Interestingly, in 2011–2012, the Bobcats won seven or only 10 % of their games, had the all-time worst winning percentage in NBA history, and sold just 77 % of available tickets to their home games.

In 2013, the franchise ranked 29th in the league with an estimated market value of $410 million, $115 million in revenue, and $64 million in player expenses. Despite these comparatively low financial amounts and a small payroll, the Bobcats have such young players as former All-Americans' Michael Kidd-Gilchrist and Kemba Walker, and veterans Al Jefferson and Josh McRoberts, who as a group, played well enough to make the postseason.

Given an opportunity, majority owner Michael Jordan may or may not move the Bobcats. Charlotte is close to his hometown of Wilmington, North Carolina, which is a major reason for him not to transfer the team to San Diego or Seattle on the west coast or to another remote location. However, with the potential to play home games in a larger market and earn greater amounts of revenue and operating income, these factors might sway him.

Some NBA officials and team owners question the long-term viability of the Charlotte Bobcats, who have never won a division title and struggle to fill seats at their home games. Nevertheless, NBA legend and North Carolina native Michael Jordan does not want a legacy of permitting his professional franchise to leave town.

Milwaukee Bucks

During five recent NBA seasons, the Milwaukee Bucks won 46 % of their games and appeared in two playoffs. Moreover, since the 2008–2009 season, their attendances at the 18,700-seat BMO Harris Bradley Center ranked 25th in the league at 15.1 thousand per game and finished in the bottom four with respect to percentage of seats filled at the arena. Recently, the Bucks sold a pathetic 78 % of their available tickets, which suggests that sports fans in Milwaukee do not care about their team.

When a handful of key players left as free agents, including guards Brandon Jennings and Monta Ellis, the Bucks suddenly had to rebuild their roster in 2013. Thus, owner Herb Kohl could eventually opt to relocate and an available option for such a move would be Seattle, Washington. This city is a larger sports market than Milwaukee with fans that, as a group, remain angry over the loss of the Supersonics. Thus, the Bucks would be welcome and receive more support in this market on the west coast. Since the franchise did not resign Jennings and Ellis, a potential move is less complicated but certainly a strategic decision.

The Bucks, who operate on an annual lease at the 26-year-old Bradley Center, are the property of former US Senator Herb Kohl. He retired from politics to devote more time to his franchise, specifically, to get a new arena built for the team. "That stands as one of those markets that without a sizable increase in local support and with an aging facility and owner, it has the characteristics one would look for in saying that's a team ripe for ownership change and quite possibly location change," said the managing director at the University of Oregon's Sports Marketing Center Paul Swangard.[6]

Kohl, however, would not likely sell the Bucks to anyone planning to move it. For example, several years ago he nixed a possible sale to Michael Jordan knowing Jordan would relocate the team to Charlotte, North Carolina. Kohl also was an NBA owner who fought hard for revenue sharing. In fact, he foresees the Bucks' future more viable in Milwaukee than previously, in part, because the team gets roughly $10 million more a year from the league's new Collective Bargaining Agreement.[7]

Western Conference

Memphis Grizzlies

During the past few seasons, the Grizzlies have established themselves as one of the best teams in the WC. They have also become one of the most vulnerable franchises in the NBA because of a change in management. Consequently, a potential move of it to Las Vegas, Seattle, or another city is a serious possibility.

The franchise's new majority owner Robert J. Pera, a founder and Chief Executive Officer of Ubiquiti Networks, is only 34-years-old. He and Denver Broncos quarterback Peyton Manning, former NBA star Penny Hardaway, and other investors including Memphis native Justin Timberlake, co-own the Grizzlies. As such, this group of relatively young but wealthy men could be prone to a drastic move. Although Timberlake much prefers to keep his hometown team in Memphis, an opportunity to move it to a new arena with a greater potential for profit could entice him and the other owners.

Although undetermined, there is a small but possible chance the Grizzlies will leave Memphis within 5–10 years after 2013. In fact, the team is a candidate for

---

[6] "It [Milwaukee Bucks] has the characteristics one would look for in saying that's a team ripe for ownership change and quite possibly location change," Swangard said in an interview with The Seattle Times. See "Time to Start Talking About a New Arena" at http://www.jsonline.com cited 27 March 2014. After 4 months of negotiation, Bucks owner Herb Kohn reportedly sold his franchise for $550 million in April 2014 to Wall Street money managers Marc Lasry and Wesley Edens. These wealthy men are lifelong basketball fans and enticed by the prospect of building a new arena for the team over the next 3 years. For more details about the deal, read Mike Spector and Juliet Chung, "Billionaires Lay Out Bucks For NBA Team," *Wall Street Journal* (17 April 2014), C3.

[7] In 2013, the Bucks ranked 30th in estimated market value at $405 million and revenue at $109 million. While the club had operating income of $11.5 million, player expenses were less than $70 million. See Kurt Badenhausen, Mike Ozanian, and Christina Settimi, "NBA Team Values: The Business of Basketball" at http://www.forbes.com cited 6 February 2014. Regarding NBA expansion in the future, *Forbes* senior sports business editor Kurt Badenhausen wrote me and declared, "I don't believe the NBA is expanding anywhere in the next 5 years. Would seem tempting with franchise values soaring, but the tradeoff is a smaller slice of TV money. Seattle is the obvious candidate for the next franchise through either expansion or relocation, but I don't think anything is imminent. Assuming the Bucks stay in Milwaukee with new ownership, I think the next most likely candidates for relocation are Atlanta and Minnesota if I had to pick two. I think both are long shots to move, but any changes in ownership down the road could trigger something."

relocation because it struggles to sellout games at the 18,911-seat FedExForum despite fielding a young, winning team. During the NBA's 2008–2009 to 2012–2013 seasons, for example, the Grizzlies ranked 24th in the league with average home attendance of 14.1 thousand per game. Despite these problems, the team has a restrictive lease with the city in which anyone who wants to move the team from Memphis must pay off bonds issued for the construction of the FedExForum.[8]

New Orleans Pelicans

During five recent NBA regular seasons, the Pelicans won 45 % of their games and appeared in two playoffs. Their attendances at the 17,000-seat Smoothie King Center were 15.1 thousand per game, which ranked 25th among teams in the league. The Pelicans also have a lease with the city through 2014 that complicates a relocation of them to another city.

After buying the team from George Shinn, the NBA sold it in 2012 to a syndicate led by New Orleans Saints owner Tom Benson. Soon thereafter, Benson signed such players as Ryan Anderson, Jrue Holiday, and then Tyreke Evans. With all-star Anthony Davis, this competitive club entertains fans at games. Thus, Benson intends to win now, in part, to rekindle the love between the city and professional basketball and thereby increase attendances at his Pelicans' home games.

As a business enterprise in 2013, the Pelicans franchise ranked 28th in estimated market value at $420 million among 30 NBA teams. In addition, the team's revenue was $115 million and operating income $11.2 million. To compare these amounts, the New York Knicks' were, respectively, equal to $1.4 billion, $287 million, and $96.3 million.

Consequently, New Orleans has challenges economically and is a difficult market for Benson's team to attract sports fans, increase gate receipts and revenue from games, and compete for division and conference titles. Although former Commissioner David Stern preferred the Pelicans remain in New Orleans, this may change if the team does not generate more interest from local and regional sports fans in Louisiana.[9]

---

[8] According to a recent financial report published in early 2014, the Grizzlies ranked 24th among all NBA teams in market value at $453 million. In addition, the club's revenue was $126 million and operating income $11.2 million. For this and other financial statistics, see the Grizzlies data in the *Forbes* article "NBA Team Values: The Business of Basketball."

[9] During April 2014, Director of Academic Programs for Sport Management at the University of San Francisco Dan Rascher forwarded me a reply to my question about expansion and relocation in the NBA. He said, "I do think that the NBA will allow either a relocation or expansion into Seattle (and maybe elsewhere like Las Vegas) in the future. First, it didn't allow the Kings to move to SEA because it didn't want a privately financed arena in SEA to set a precedent. The league does want a team there though. Also, as profits continue to rise (and population continues to grow) in the NBA, the marginal city will become viable and the league will want to cash it on the expansion fee." Regarding global expansion by the NBA, Professor Rascher remarked, "I don't think the international divisions will work too well. I can see the winner of the NBA maybe 1 day playing a three-game series against the winner of the Euroleague or something, but not league integration. There could be brand extension where the NBA brands the Euro league, but true within-season games (other than some token games) against Europe still seems remote."

League Mergers

After these professional leagues combined their operations in 1949 and then changed as organizations, ten teams from the former Basketball Association of America (BAA) and six from the National Basketball League (NBL) joined the NBA. Among the previous group were the Boston Celtics and New York Knickerbockers while most NBL teams folded or moved to different cities after one or more regular seasons in the NBA. Then 21 years later, the ABA Denver Nuggets, Indiana Pacers, New Jersey Nets, and San Antonio Spurs shifted to the NBA after the two leagues merged and formed one organization.

Other than the NBA Development League, several local/regional professional and semiprofessional basketball leagues operate in small and midsized sports markets of America. Although they are not a threat to seriously challenge, intimidate, or worry the NBA, their teams exist for 1 or more years and play scheduled games in arenas and various other venues in cities across the US.

To identify them, some current or former minor groups in the sport are the Central Basketball League, International Basketball League, and Premier Basketball League. Furthermore, three short-season semiprofessional leagues are the Atlantic Coast Professional Basketball League, Eastern Basketball Alliance, and United Basketball League. While two or more of these leagues may consolidate in the future and schedule their teams to perform in games during regular seasons, they will not influence or have any major impact on the decisions, strategies, and tactics of the NBA.

Because it is the world's premier basketball organization, the NBA may negotiate and sign an agreement, establish an alliance, or otherwise maintain a relationship with one or more foreign leagues in order to become even more popular, powerful, and rich. Abroad, the biggest and best leagues are Spain's Liga ACB, Greek's Heba A1, Argentina's Liga Nacional De Basquet, Italy's Liga Basket Serie A, and the Turkish Basketball League, Chinese Basketball Association, and French Pro A League.[10]

---

[10] Canada's National Basketball League (CNBL) opened in 2011 with seven teams. The Halifax Rainmen, Saint John Mill Rats, and Quebec Kebs moved from the country's Premier Basketball League to the CNBL while the other four were expansion teams including the London Lightning, Moncton Miracles, Summerside Storm, and Oshawa Power. For the 2012–2013 NBL season, the Windsor Express joined the CNBL while the Kebs relocated to Laval. However, before the Kebs played any games there, the league terminated them after issues with their management. The league then replaced the Kebs with a team based in Quebec called the Montreal Jazz. In the same season, the league announced Ottawa Skyhawks as a new team for 2013–2014. Following the 2012–2013 season, the Oshawa Power relocated to Mississauga and renamed the Mississauga Power while the Summerside Storm moved to Charlottetown to become the Island Storm. During August 2013, the CNBL Board of Governors announced that the Jazz would participate in the 2013–2014 season after failing to secure new ownership. See "NBL Canada Basketball (Men)." http://www.usbasket.com cited 27 March 2014, and "NBL Canada: It's Showtime." http://www.nblcanada.com cited 27 March 2014.

Several teams in foreign basketball leagues are globally competitive and won Olympic medals, Euroleague titles, and FIBA championships. While NBA clubs recruit and sign contracts with players from clubs in international leagues, many outstanding US college and university graduates and professional athletes need more experience, skills, and training in basketball. Thus, they join, for example, such well-known foreign teams as La Roja in Spain, Panathinaikos in Greece, or Lottomatica in Italy.

Based on the status of current sports, it is unlikely another competitive, prominent, and successful professional basketball association or league will emerge in America before 2025 and challenge the NBA. Simply put, the BAA–NBL and ABA–NBA mergers were the results of too many professional basketball leagues in America's sports markets and their failure to coexist and thrive for decades as independent organizations.

Appendix

Table A2.1 NBA expansion franchises before 1976, team performances, first season

Year	Team	Record	Rank (GB)	Attendance	Points	
					For	Against
1961	Chicago Packers	18–62	5th (36)	NA	110	119
1966	Chicago Bulls	33–48	4th (11)	4,772	113	116
1967	San Diego Rockets	15–67	6th (41)	4,067	112	121
1967	Seattle Supersonics	21–61	5th (33)	8,823	107	114
1968	Milwaukee Bucks	27–55	7th (30)	5,942	110	115
1968	Phoenix Suns	16–66	7th (39)	4,335	111	120
1970	Buffalo Braves	22–60	4th (30)	4,977	105	112
1970	Cleveland Cavaliers	15–67	4th (27)	3,518	102	113
1970	Portland Trail Blazers	29–53	5th (19)	6,135	115	120
1974	New Orleans Jazz	23–59	5th (37)	4,955	101	109

Note: Year is the expansion year and these teams' first regular season in the league. Record is teams' number of wins–losses. Rank is their place in a division. GB is games behind the leading team in their division. Attendance is teams' home attendances per games in thousands. Points are the average number scored by them and their opponents. NA is Not Available
Source: "Teams" at http://www.basketball-reference.com cited 5 February 2014, and "Teams Websites" at http://www.nba.com cited 5 February 2014

Table A2.2 NBA expansions before 1976, population data, selected years

Year	Expansion site	Population		Population rank	
		City	Metropolitan area	City	Metropolitan area
1961	Chicago (IL)	3,550,404	6,220,913	2	3
1966	Chicago (IL)	3,369,359	6,978,947	2	3
1967	San Diego (CA)	696,769	1,357,854	14	23
1967	Seattle (WA)	530,831	1,421,869	22	17
1968	Milwaukee (WI)	717,372	1,403,887	12	19

(continued)

F.P. Jozsa Jr., *National Basketball Association Strategies*,
SpringerBriefs in Economics 84, DOI 10.1007/978-3-319-10058-6

Table A2.2 (continued)

Year	Expansion site	Population		Population rank	
		City	Metropolitan area	City	Metropolitan area
1968	Phoenix (AZ)	581,562	968,487	20	34
1970	Buffalo (NY)	462,768	1,349,211	28	24
1970	Cleveland (OH)	750,879	2,064,194	10	12
1970	Portland (OR)	380,620	1,009,129	36	33
1974	New Orleans (LA)	593,471	1,046,470	19	31

Note: NBA is National Basketball Association. States are Illinois (IL), California (CA), Washington (WA), Wisconsin (WI), Arizona (AZ), New York (NY), Ohio (OH), Oregon (OR), and Louisiana (LA). Population is in thousands
Source: US population data is from the 1962 and 1972 *World Almanac and Book of Facts*

Table A3.1 NBA expansion franchises from 1976, team performances, first season

Year	Team	Record	Rank (GB)	Attendance	Points	
					For	Against
1980	Dallas Mavericks	15–67	6th (37)	7,788	101	109
1988	Charlotte Hornets	20–62	6th (32)	23,172	104	113
1988	Miami Heat	15–67	6th (36)	14,945	97	109
1989	Orlando Magic	18–64	7th (41)	15,060	110	119
1989	Minnesota Timberwolves	22–60	6th (34)	26,160	95	99
1995	Toronto Raptors	21–61	8th (51)	23,179	97	105
1995	Vancouver Grizzlies	15–67	7th (44)	17,183	89	99
2004	Charlotte Bobcats	18–64	4th (41)	14,431	94	100

Note: Year is the expansion year and these teams' first regular season in the league. Record is teams' number of wins–losses. Rank is their place in a division. GB is games behind the leading team in their division. Attendance is teams' home attendances per game in thousands. Points are the average numbers scored by them and their opponents
Source: "Teams" at http://www.basketball-reference.com cited 5 February 2014, and "Teams Websites" at http://www.nba.com cited 5 February 2014

Table A3.2 NBA expansions from 1976, population data, selected years

Year	Expansion site	Population		Population Rank	
		City	Metropolitan area	City	Metropolitan area
1980	Dallas (TX)	904,078	2,964,342	7	8
1988	Charlotte (NC)	395,934	1,162,093	35	34
1988	Miami (FL)	358,548	3,192,582	46	11
1989	Orlando (FL)	164,693	1,072,748	NR	37
1989	Minneapolis (MN)	368,383	2,464,124	42	16
1995	Toronto (Ontario)	2,385,421	4,263,757	1	1
1995	Vancouver (BC)	514,008	1,831,665	8	3
2004	Charlotte (NC)	540,828	1,499,293	26	34

Note: NBA is National Basketball Association. Population is in thousands. The symbols are Texas (TX), North Carolina (NC), Florida (FL), Minnesota (MN), and British Columbia (BC). Located in Ontario Province, Toronto was Canada's largest city and metropolitan area in 1995. NR means not ranked
Source: US population data is from the 1982, 1992, and 2002 *World Almanac and Book of Facts*. Canadian data is from the *Census of Canada* website http://www.12.statcan.gc.ca

Table A4.1 NBA team relocations before 1976, performances, selected years/seasons

Year	Team relocations		Seasons		Playoffs		Championships	
	Before	After	Before	After	Before	After	Before	After
1951	Tri-Cities Blackhawks	Milwaukee Hawks	2	4	1	0	0	0
1955	Milwaukee Hawks	St. Louis Hawks	4	13	0	12	0	11
1957	Fort Wayne Pistons	Detroit Pistons	8	57	8	32	4	17
1957	Rochester Royals	Cincinnati Royals	8	15	7	7	3	0
1960	Minneapolis Lakers	Los Angeles Lakers	11	54	11	49	9	64
1962	Philadelphia Warriors	SF Warriors	13	9	12	4	5	6
1963	Chicago Zephyrs	Baltimore Bullets	2	10	0	8	0	4
1963	Syracuse Nationals	Philadelphia 76ers	14	51	14	33	4	16
1968	St. Louis Hawks	Atlanta Hawks	13	46	12	29	11	4
1971	San Diego Rockets	Houston Rockets	4	43	1	27	0	10
1971	SF Warriors	Golden State Warriors	9	43	4	14	6	6
1972	Cincinnati Royals	KC-Omaha Kings	15	13	7	5	0	1
1973	Baltimore Bullets	Cap./Wash. Bull./Wiz.	10	41	8	18	4	7

Note: NBA is National Basketball Association. Year is when teams' moved to their new home site. Seasons are teams' number of regular seasons at their pre-move and post-move sites. Playoffs are number of appearances. Championships include division and conference titles and league championships. The teams' names and/or nicknames are San Francisco (SF), Kansas City (KC), Capital (Cap.), Washington (Wash.), Bullets (Bull.), and Wizards (Wiz.)
Source: "NBA Teams Websites" at http://www.nba.com cited 5 February 2014
"Rodney D. Fort's Sports Business Data" at http://sites.google.com cited 5 February 2014, "Teams" at http://www.basketball-reference.com cited 5 February 2014, and "Teams" at http://www.sportsencyclopdia.com cited 12 February 2014

Table A4.2 NBA team relocations before 1976, population data, selected years

Year	Before	After	Population		Population rank	
			Before	After	Before	After
1951	Tri-Cities	Milwaukee Hawks	NA	863,937	NA	16
1955	Milwaukee Hawks	St. Louis Hawks	1,194,290	2,060,103	17	9
1957	Fort Wayne Pistons	Detroit Piston	232,196	3,762,360	113	5

(continued)

Table A4.2 (continued)

Year	Before	After	Population		Population rank	
			Before	After	Before	After
1957	Rochester Royals	Cincinnati Royals	586,387	1,071,624	34	21
1960	Minneapolis Lakers	Los Angeles Lakers	1,482,030	6,742,696	14	2
1962	Philadelphia Warriors	SF Warriors	4,342,897	2,783,459	4	6
1963	Chicago Zephyrs	Baltimore Bullets	6,220,913	1,727,023	3	12
1963	Syracuse Nationals	Philadelphia 76ers	563,781	4,342,897	51	4
1968	St. Louis Hawks	Atlanta Hawks	2,363,017	1,390,164	10	20
1971	San Diego Rockets	Houston Rockets	1,357,854	1,985,031	23	13
1971	SF Warriors	Golden State Warriors	3,104,519	3,104,519	6	6
1972	Cincinnati Royals	KC-Omaha Kings	1,384,911	1,256,649	21	26
1973	Baltimore Bullets	Cap./Wash. Bull./Wiz.	2,070,670	2,861,123	11	7

Note: NBA is National Basketball Association. Year is when teams' moved to their new home site. The teams' names and/or nicknames are San Francisco (SF), Kansas City (KC), Capital (Cap.), Washington (Wash.), Bullets (Bull.), and Wizards (Wiz.). Population is in thousands for metropolitan areas. San Francisco and Oakland are in the same metropolitan area

Source: Populations and population ranks are from editions of the *World Almanac and Book of Facts*

Table A5.1 NBA team relocations from 1976, performances, selected years/seasons

Year	Team relocations		Seasons		Playoffs		Championships	
	Before	After	Before	After	Before	After	Before	After
1977	New York Nets	New Jersey Nets	1	35	0	16	0	6
1978	Buffalo Braves	San Diego Clippers	8	6	3	0	0	0
1979	New Orleans Jazz	Utah Jazz	5	35	0	25	0	10
1984	San Diego Clippers	Los Angeles Clippers	6	30	0	7	0	2
1985	Kansas City Kings	Sacramento Kings	13	29	5	10	1	2
2001	Vancouver Grizzlies	Memphis Grizzlies	6	13	0	7	0	0

(continued)

Table A5.1 (continued)

Year	Team relocations		Seasons		Playoffs		Championships	
	Before	After	Before	After	Before	After	Before	After
2002	Charlotte Hornets	NO Hornets/ Pelicans	15	12	7	5	0	1
2008	Seattle Supersonics	Oklahoma City Thunder	41	6	21	5	10	5
2012	New Jersey Nets	Brooklyn Nets	35	2	16	2	6	0

Note: NBA is National Basketball Association. The slash (/) indicates change in nickname. Year is when teams moved to their new home site and the first NBA season there. Seasons are teams' number of regular seasons at their pre-move and post-move sites. Playoffs are number of their appearances. Championships include their division and conference titles and league championships. NO is New Orleans. Population data is for metropolitan areas
Source: "NBA Teams Websites" at http://www.nba.com cited 5 February 2014, "Rodney D. Fort's Sports Business Data" at http://sites.google.com cited 5 February 2014, "Teams" at http://www.basketball-reference.com cited 5 February 2014, and "Teams" at http://www.sportsencyclopdia.com cited 12 February 2014

Table A5.2 NBA team relocations from 1976, population data, selected years

Year	Before	After	Population		Population rank	
			Before	After	Before	After
1977	New York Nets	New Jersey Nets	9,080,777	594,984	1	65
1978	Buffalo Braves	San Diego Clippers	1,241,434	1,859,623	31	20
1979	New Orleans Jazz	Utah Jazz	1,183,606	935,280	33	40
1984	San Diego Clippers	Los Angeles Clippers	1,859,623	7,445,721	20	2
1985	Kansas City Kings	Sacramento Kings	1,566,280	1,481,102	25	26
2001	Vancouver Grizzlies	Memphis Grizzlies	1,986,965	1,135,614	NA	44
2002	Charlotte Hornets	NO Hornets/ Pelicans	1,499,293	1,337,726	34	35
2008	Seattle Supersonics	Oklahoma City Thunder	3,439,809	1,252,987	15	44
2012	New Jersey Nets	Brooklyn Nets	18,897,109	18,897,109	1	1

Note: NBA is National Basketball Association. The slash (/) indicates change in nickname. Year is when teams moved to their new home site and the first NBA season there. Population is in thousands. NO is New Orleans. Except for Vancouver, the population data is for US metropolitan statistical areas. After relocating in 1977, the Nets had a site in New Brunswick, New Jersey. If it were a US metropolitan statistical area in 2001, Vancouver's population ranked between twenty-third (Portland) and twenty-fourth (Cincinnati). NA means Not Applicable. As home sites of the Nets, Newark and Brooklyn were in the same metropolitan statistical area in 2012
Source: Population data is from editions of the *World Almanac and Book of Facts*

Table A6.1 BAA, NBL teams in NBA, population data, 1949

Team	Population		Population rank	
	City	Metropolitan area	City	Metropolitan area
BAA				
Baltimore Bullets	940,205	1,320,754	6	12
Boston Celtics	790,863	2,354,507	10	6
Chicago Stags	3,606,436	5,475,535	2	2
Fort Wayne Pistons	132,840	182,903	70	98
Minneapolis Lakers	517,277	1,107,366	17	13
New York Knickerbockers	7,835,099	8,392,986	1	1
Philadelphia Warriors	2,064,794	3,660,676	3	4
Rochester Royals	331,252	484,877	31	35
St. Louis Bombers	852,623	1,673,467	8	9
Washington Capitols	797,670	1,457,601	9	10
NBL				
Anderson Packers	46,820	NA	NA	NA
Denver Nuggets	412,856	2,560,361	24	26
Sheboygan Redskins	42,365	NA	NA	NA
Syracuse Nationals	220,067	340,875	47	49
Tri-Cities Blackhawks	NA	NA	NA	NA
Waterloo Hawks	65,198	99,580	NA	151

Note: Teams played in the Basketball Association of America (BAA) or National Basketball League (NBL). Population is in thousands. Data is not available (NA)
Source: Population data is from editions of the *World Almanac and Book of Facts*

Table A7.1 ABA team relocations and performances, selected years/seasons

Year	Team relocations		Seasons		Playoffs		Championships	
	Before	After	Before	After	Before	After	Before	After
1968	Anaheim Amigos	Los Angeles Stars	1	3	0	1	0	0
1968	New Jersey Americans	New York Nets	1	8	1	7	0	4
1968	Pittsburgh Pipers	Minnesota Pipers	1	1	1	1	2	0
1968	Minnesota Muskies	Miami Floridians	1	4	1	3	0	0
1969	Minnesota Pipers	Pittsburgh P/C	1	3	1	0	0	0
1969	Oakland Oaks	Washington Capitols	2	1	1	1	2	0
1969	Houston Mavericks	Carolina Cougars	2	5	1	3	0	1
1970	Los Angeles Stars	Utah Stars	3	6	1	5	0	4
1970	New Orleans Bucs	Memphis Pros/T/S	3	5	2	2	1	0

(continued)

Table A7.1 (continued)

Year	Team relocations		Seasons		Playoffs		Championships	
	Before	After	Before	After	Before	After	Before	After
1970	Washington Capitols	Virginia Squires	1	6	1	4	0	1
1973	Dallas/Texas Chaparrals	San Antonio Spurs	6	3	5	3	0	0
1974	Carolina Cougars	St. Louis Spirits	5	2	3	1	1	0

Note: ABA is American Basketball Association. Bucs are Buccaneers. P/C is Pipers/Condors. T/S is Tams/Sounds. Seasons and Playoffs are the number at the pre-move and post-move sites. Championships include division titles and ABA championships

Source: Frank P. Jozsa Jr., *The National Basketball Association: Business, Organization and Strategy* (Singapore: World Scientific, 2011), and James Quirk and Rodney D. Fort, *Pay Dirt: The Business of Professional Team Sports* (Princeton, NJ: Princeton University Press, 1992)

Table A7.2 ABA team relocations, population data, selected years

Year	Before	After	Population		Population rank	
			Before	After	Before	After
1968	Anaheim Amigos	Los Angeles Stars	1,420,386	7,032,075	18	2
1968	New Jersey Americans	New York Nets	11,528,386	11,528,649	1	1
1968	Pittsburgh Pipers	Minnesota Pipers	2,401,245	1,813,647	9	15
1968	Minnesota Muskies	Miami Floridians	1,813,647	1,267,792	15	25
1969	Minnesota Pipers	Pittsburgh P/C	1,813,647	2,401,245	15	9
1069	Oakland Oaks	Washington Caps	3,109,519	2,861,123	6	7
1969	Houston Mavericks	Carolina Cougars	1,985,031	409,370	13	73
1970	Los Angeles Stars	Utah Stars	7,032,075	557,635	2	57
1970	New Orleans Bucs	Memphis Pros/T/S	1,046,470	770,120	31	42
1970	Washington Caps	Virginia Squires	2,861,123	518,319	7	65
1973	Dallas/Texas Chaps	San Antonio Spurs	1,555,950	864,014	16	38
1974	Carolina Cougars	St. Louis Spirits	409,370	2,363,017	73	10

Note: Abbreviations are American Basketball Association (ABA), Buccaneers (Bucs), Pipers/Condors (P/C), Tams/Sounds (T/S), Capitols (Caps), and Chaparrals (Chaps). Population is for US metropolitan statistical areas in hundreds of thousands. In 1968, the Americans and Nets were in the same area

Source: Population data is from editions of the *World Almanac and Book of Facts*

Table A8.1 Potential NBA expansion sites, population data, 2014

Expansion site (State)	Population		Population rank	
	City	Metropolitan area	City	Metropolitan area
Baltimore (MD)	621,342	2,753,149	26	20
Jacksonville (FL)	836,507	1,377,850	12	40
Kansas City (MO)	464,310	2,038,724	37	30
Las Vegas (NV)	596,424	2,000,759	31	31
Louisville (KY)	605,110	1,251,351	27	43
Nashville (TN)	624,496	1,726,693	25	36
Pittsburgh (PA)	306,211	2,360,733	61	22
San Diego (CA)	1,338,348	3,177,063	8	17
Seattle (WA)	634,535	3,552,157	22	15
St. Louis (MO)	318,172	2,795,794	58	19

Note: NBA is National Basketball Association. Population is in hundreds of thousands. US states are Maryland (MD), Florida (FL), Missouri (MO), Nevada (NV), Kentucky (KY), Tennessee (TN), Pennsylvania (PA), California (CA), and Washington (WA)

Source: Population data is from the 2014 *World Almanac and Book of Facts*

Bibliography

Articles

Appleman, Jake. "Kings Continue to Call Sacramento Home, For Now." *New York Times* (23 November 2012): 10.
Araton, Harvey. "Grizzlies' Relocation Reveals the N.B.A's Fault Lines." *New York Times* (25 March 2001): 11.
Aron, Jaime. "2 Owners Like Vegas For Expansion Team." *Charlotte Observer* (23 January 2004): 4C.
Attner, Paul. "How Professional Sports Governs Expansion Will Mean Success or Failure for 21st Century." *The Sporting News* (18 March 1991): 13–19.
Ball, J.R. "Is the State Big Enough For Both of Them?" *Greater Baton Rouge Business Report* (12 March 2002): 38.
Ballard, Chris. "The NBA's Trail of Tears Cheers." *Sports Illustrated* (4 March 2013): 56.
"Basketball." *Sports Illustrated* (17 February 1977): 116.
"Basketball NBA Off to India." *New Zealand Herald* (8 May 2008): 1.
Belson, Ken. "Two Groups Present Pitches For Kings." *New York Times* (4 April 2013): 15.
"BET Founder Bob Johnson First Black Majority Owner of Sports Franchise." *Jet* (13 January 2003): 48.
"BET's Founder Wins Franchise." *New York Times* (18 December 2002): D3.
Biderman, David. "Staples Stays in LA in Deal of a Lifetime." *Wall Street Journal* (29 October 2009): D10.
Bradsher, Keith. "New Push Into China by N.B.A." *New York Times* (19 September 2007): 1.
Branch, Dallas, Jr. "The Charlotte Bobcats: (Re) Launching a New (Old) NBA Franchise." *Sport Marketing Quarterly* (2008): 57–62.
Brewer, Jerry. "Rocky Start in China's Rudimentary Basketball League." *Seattle Times* (20 January 2008): 1.
Broussard, Chris. "A Possible Challenge to Knicks' Supremacy." *New York Times* (22 January 2004): D8.
Carry, Peter. "A War is Over, and the Shooting Starts." *Sports Illustrated* (25 October 1971): 37.
———. "Indiana Has a Hot New Poet." *Sports Illustrated* (20 April 1970): 55.
———. "Meanwhile, Back at the Merge." *Sports Illustrated* (24 May 1971): 68.
"Charlotte Bidders Are Heard." *New York Times* (17 December 2002): D6.
"China Tries For a Slam Dunk With NBA." *MX* (15 January 2008): 1.
"Chinese Investors to Take Minority Stake in Cleveland Cavaliers." *Wall Street Journal* (26 May 2009): B10.

F.P. Jozsa Jr., *National Basketball Association Strategies*,
SpringerBriefs in Economics 84, DOI 10.1007/978-3-319-10058-6

"Clippers to Anaheim?" *Washington Post News Feed* (3 June 1996): C7.
Cook, Kevin, and Mark Mravic. "Borderline Call." *Sports Illustrated* (4 October 1999): 34.
Cohen, Jackie. "Las Vegas Plans New Arena With Eye Towards Luring a Pro Team." *Bond Buyer* (24 July 2006): 6.
Creamer, Robert. "Scorecard." *Sports Illustrated* (30 November 1970): 11.
Crouse, Karen. "Welcome Mat is Not Assured For Nets in Brooklyn." *New York Times* (26 February 2007): D1–D3.
"Deal Allows the Sonics to Leave Seattle For Oklahoma City." *New York Times* (3 July 2008): 6.
Deford, Frank. "Buy a Basketball Franchise and Join the War." *Sports Illustrated* (2 February 1970): 40.
———. "Dribbling on the Verge of the Merger." *Sports Illustrated* (9 August 1971): 42.
———. "Merger, Madness and Maravich." *Sports Illustrated* (6 April 1970): 28.
———. "One Last Hurrah in Hyannis." *Sports Illustrated* (28 June 1976): 64.
———. "Scorecard." *Sports Illustrated* (17 May 1971): 15.
Edelman, Marc, and Brian Doyle. "Antitrust and 'Free Movement' Risks of Expanding U.S. Professional Sports Leagues Into Europe." *Northwestern Journal of International Law & Business* (2009): 403–428.
Eisenberg, Daniel. "The NBA's Global Game Plan." *Time Europe* (31 March 2003): 115.
Friedman, Nick, *et.al.* "Basketball Without Borders." *Sports Illustrated* (July 2004): 20.
Glick, J. "Professional Sports Franchise Movements and the Sherman Act: When and Where Teams Should be Able to Move." *Santa Clara Law Review 23* (Winter 1983): 55–94.
Graf, Christine. "Basketball Without Borders." *Faces* (October 2006): 24–27.
Henderson, Rick. "Building Buzz." *Reason* (July 1997): 17.
"Hornets, City Officials Agree to Win-Win Practice Site Deal." *New Orleans City Business* (24 January 2005): 26.
Jenkins, Lee, Richard O'Brien, Mark Bechtel, and Mark Beech. "The Only Game in Town." *Sports Illustrated* (6 May 2013): 15.
Johnson, Arthur T. "The Sports Franchise Relocation Issue and Public Policy Responses." In: Arthur T. Johnson and James H. Frey, eds., *Government and Sport: The Public Policy Issues*. Totowa, N.J.: Rowman and Allanheld, 1985.
Johnson, Chuck. "Game Grabbing Globe: Ilgauskas Says." *USA Today* (11 June 2007): 1.
Kennedy, Ray. "A Celtic Rookie Puts It Together." *Sports Illustrated* (25 October 1976): 94.
King, Pat. "Las Vegas an Unlikely Fit For the NBA." *Las Vegas Business Press* (19 February 2001): 13.
Kirkpatrick, Curry. "A Season For All Men." *Sports Illustrated* (25 October 1976): 34.
Knightly, Arnold M. "Follow the Bouncing Ball to Vegas." *Business Press* (23 January 2006): 12.
Lazaroff, D. "The Antitrust Implications of Franchise Relocation Restrictions in Professional Sports." *Fordham Law Review 53* (November 1984): 157–220.
Longman, Jere. "Hornets Thrive Amid Empty Seats in New Orleans." *New York Times* (12 February 2008): 1.
Markovits, Benjamin. "A New Global Game?" *New Statesman* (19 January 2009): 28.
Marshall, Samantha. "NBA's Big Plans Hinge on Beijing." *Crain's New York Business* (7 July 2008): 3, 6.
McCallum, Jack. "Hello, New Orleans!" *Sports Illustrated* (11 November 2002): 76.
Means, Jason, and John Nauright. "Going Global: The NBA Sets Its Sights on Africa." *International Journal of Sports Marketing & Sponsorship* (October 2007): 40–50.
"NBA China to Manage Beijing Arena During and After Olympics." *Canadian Press* (31 January 2008): 1.
"NBA Names Investors in China Venture: New League is Possible." *Wall Street Journal* (15 January 2008): B5.
"NBA Seeks to Double Its Chinese Operations." *Wall Street Journal* (7 August 2006): B3.
"No Way! To San Jose!" *Washington Post News Feed* (31 March 1996): D6.
Osnos, Evan. "NBA Targets Biggest Prize in Sports: Chinese Market." *Chicago Tribune* (30 October 2005): 1.

Pells, Eddie. "China is a Big-Bucks Proposition For American Sports Leagues." *Marketing News* (1 September 2007): 32.
Povtak, Tim. "NBA Going Full Force in Tapping the Vast China Market." *Orlando Sentinel* (17 October 2007): 1.
Quirk, James. "An Economic Analysis of Team Movements in Professional Sports." *Law and Contemporary Problems 38* (Winter/Spring 1973): 42–66.
Ramsey, David. "Football is America's Game, But NBA is the World's Game." *Colorado Spring Gazette* (25 September 2008): 1.
Rascher, Daniel, and Heather Rascher. "NBA Expansion and Relocation: A Viability Study of Various Cities." *Journal of Sport Management* (2004): 274–294.
Rhoden, Bill. "ABA Superstars Join the NBA." *Ebony* (January 1977): 88–89.
Robbins, Liz. "Traveling Music For the Hornets." *New York Times* (7 July 2002): 6.
Ronberg, Gary. "Tossing Bombs Into the Hoops." *Sports Illustrated* (22 September 1969): 30.
Rozin, Skip. "Growing Pains: The Evolution of Expansion." *Sport* (December 1994): 10.
Sabino, David, and Mark Bechtel. "Expansion Plan." *Sports Illustrated* (28 June 2004): 32.
Sandomir, Richard. "Founder of TV Network Becomes First Black Owner in Major Sports." *New York Times* (19 December 2002): A1.
———. "N.B.A. Board Approves Jordan's Purchase of the Bobcats." *New York Times* (18 March 2010): 18.
———. "Sonics Given Approval to Move to Oklahoma." *New York Times* (19 April 2008): 2.
Schoenfeld, Bruce. "Where the Thunder Comes Dribbling Down the Plain." *New York Times Magazine* (26 October 2008): 61.
"SI Players NBA Poll." *Sports Illustrated* (8 August 2011): 11.
Song, Wang. "The NBA's 'China Derby.'" *China Today* (May 2008): 54–56.
"Sonics' Bid to Leave Seattle Gets League Nod." *Wall Street Journal* (21 April 2008): A10.
"Sonics the Most Likely to Move." *Charlotte Observer* (19 February 2006): 14C.
Spector, Mike, and Juliet Chung, "Billionaires Lay Out Bucks For NBA Team," *Wall Street Journal* (17 April 2014): C3.
Speizer, Irwin. "Shinn Given City a Surprise Boost." *Business North Carolina* (December 2002): 10.
"Spurs Kicking." *Washington Post News Feed* (2 February 1996): C5.
Stone, David. "Stern Sets His Sights Overseas." *Basketball Digest* (May 2002): 3.
"The Body Snatchers." *Time* (12 April 1971): 66.
"The Buzzing Sound." *New Orleans CityBusiness* (21 January 2002): 26.
"The Nomad Nets." *New York Times* (22 January 2004): D7.
Thomsen, Ian. "FIBA Not Thrilled About NBA's Plan." *Sports Illustrated* (25 February 2002): 75.
———. "Looking For a Clean Break." *Sports Illustrated* (29 March 2004): 85.
———. "New Home Won't End Woes." *Sports Illustrated* (9 April 2001): 83.
———. "On the Block?" *Sports Illustrated* (6 February 2006): 109.
Tsumura, Howard. "Vancouver." *Sporting News* (30 April 2001): 52.
Wise, Mike. "New Owners of Grizzlies Have Ties With St. Louis." *New York Times* (24 September 1999): D5.
Arthur T. Johnson and James H. Frey, eds., *Government and Sport: The Public Policy Issues*. Totowa, N.J.: Rowman and Allanheld, 1985.

Books

Bjarkman, Peter C. *The Encyclopedia of Pro Basketball Team Histories* (New York, NY: Carroll & Graf, 1994).
Grasso, John. *Historical Dictionary of Basketball* (Lanham, MD: Scarecrow Press, 2011).
Hubbard, Jan. *The Official NBA Encyclopedia* (New York, NY: Doubleday, 2000).
Johnson, Arthur T., and James H. Frey, eds. *Government and Sport: The Public Policy Issues* (Totowa, N.J.: Rowman and Allanheld, 1985).

Jozsa, Frank P., Jr. *The National Basketball Association: Business, Organization and Strategy* (Singapore: World Scientific, 2011).
Jozsa, Frank P., Jr., and John J. Guthrie Jr. *Relocating Teams and Expanding Leagues in Professional Sports: How the Major Leagues Respond to Market Conditions* (Westport, CT: Quorum Books, 1999).
Kirchberg, Connie. *Hoop Love: A History of the National Basketball Association* (Jefferson, NC: McFarland, 2007).
Koppett, Leonard. *Total Basketball: The Ultimate Basketball Encyclopedia* (Wilmington, DE: Sport Classic Books, 2004).
Nelson, Murray R. *The National Basketball League: A History, 1935–1949* (Jefferson, NC: McFarland, 2009).
Peterson, Robert W. *Cages to Jump Shots: Pro Basketball's Early Years* (New York, NY: Oxford University Press, 1990).
Pluto, Terry. *Loose Balls: The Short, Wild Life of the American Basketball Association* (New York, NY: Simon & Schuster, 2007).
Quirk, James, and Rodney D. Fort. *Pay Dirt: The Business of Professional Team Sports* (Princeton, NJ: Princeton University Press, 1992).
Rosen, Charles. *The First Tip-Off: The Incredible Story of the Birth of the NBA* (New York, NY: McGraw-Hill, 2008).
Shropshire, Kenneth L. *The Sports Franchise Game: Cities in Pursuit of Sports Franchises, Events, Stadiums, and Arenas* (Philadelphia, PA: University of Pennsylvania Press, 1995).
Smith, Ron, Ira Winderman, and Mary Schmitt Boyer. *The Complete Encyclopedia of Basketball* (London, England: Carlton, 2001).
Strom, Earl. *Being in Charge: My Five Decades in the NBA* (New York, NY: Simon & Schuster, 1990).
World Almanac and Book of Facts (New York, NY: Simon & Schuster, 2014).
Wright, Kyle. *The NBA From Top to Bottom: A History of the NBA, From the No. 1 Team Through No. 1,153* (Bloomington, IN: iUniverse, Inc., 2007).

Dissertations

Jozsa, Frank P., Jr. "An Economic Analysis of Franchise Relocation and League Expansion in Professional Team Sports, 1950–1975." Ph.D. diss., Georgia State University, 1977.

Government Publications

Rosenberg, Morton. "Proposed Sports Relocation Legislation: Background and Legal Implications." Washington, D.C.: American Law Division, Congressional Research Service. The Library of Congress, 1985.

Internet Sources

"A Chronology of the Teams in the NBA." http://www.nba.com cited 16 April 2014.
"American Basketball Association (1967–1977)." http://www.hoopedia.nba.com cited 20 August 2009.
"BAA/NBL Merger." http://www.n-c-systems.com cited 27 August 2005.

"BAA Teams." http://www.nbahoopsonline.com cited 3 March 2014.
Badenhausen, Kurt, Mike Ozanian, and Christina Settimi. "NBA Team Values: The Business of Basketball." http://www.forbes.com cited 6 February 2014.
"Basketball History." http://www.history-of-basketball.com cited 20 September 2005.
Bloom, Howard. "Welcome to Franchise Relocation Hell——the Seattle Sonics." http://www.sportsbusinessnews.com cited 5 November 2007.
Carry, Peter. "Having a Ball With the ABA." http://www.sportsillustrated.com cited 18 March 2014.
Condotta, Bob. "Which Struggling NBA Teams Could be Next on Seattle's Target List." http://www.seattletimes.com cited 22 March 2014.
"Could Las Vegas be the Next NBA City?" http://www.nba.fanhouse.com cited 30 October 2009.
Cour, Jim. "Sonics Looking at Arena Alternatives." http://www.netscape.sports.com cited 1 February 2006.
Garcia, Art. "Preseason Games at Home, Abroad Expand NBA's Global Reach." http://www.nba.com cited 5 October 2009.
"Global Games to Tip Off in 2014–15 Preseason on 3 Continents." http://www.nba.com cited 16 April 2014.
"History of Basketball." http://www.library.think.quest.org cited 24 August 2009.
"Is Expansion Good or Bad For the NBA?" http://www.espn.go.com cited 15 April 2014.
"Is the Most-Relocated Franchise in Sports Moving Again?" http;//www.sportsblogmovement.wordpress.com cited 16 April 2014.
Leroux, Ted. "Milwaukee Bucks Destined to Relocate to Seattle or Las Vegas." http://www.bleacherreport.com cited 23 March 2014.
"National Basketball Association (NBA) History." http://www.rauzulusstreet.com cited 12 August 2005.
"National Basketball League (NBL) Teams." http://www.rauzulusstreet.com cited 31 July 2009.
"NBA & ABA Team Index." http://www.basketball-reference.com cited 16 April 2014.
"NBA Growth Timetable." http://www.basketball.com cited 17 September 2005.
"NBA Returning to London For Regular Season Matchup." http://www.nba.com cited 21 March 2014.
"NBA Team Values: The Business of Basketball." http://www.forbes.com cited 12 February 2014.
"NBA Teams Websites." http://www.nba.com cited 5 February 2014.
"NBL Canada Basketball (Men)." http://www.usbasket.com cited 27 March 2014.
"NBL Canada: It's Showtime." http://www.nblcanada.com cited 27 March 2014.
Ogden, Maxwell. "5 NBA Teams Most Likely to Relocate to Seattle Before David Stern Retires." http://www.bleacherreport.com cited 22 March 2014.
"Professional Basketball Leagues." http://apbr.org cited 27 August 2009.
"Remember the ABA: Team Histories & Fan Memories." http://www.remembertheaba.com cited 12 March 2014.
"Rodney D. Fort's Sports Business Data." http://sites.google.com cited 5 February 2014.
Sefko, Eddie. "Mark Cuban: NBA Expansion Will Happen Before Relocation, If the Price is Right." http://www.mavsblogdallasnews.com cited 14 April 2014.
Smith, Tom. "How Did I Get Here? A History of Franchise Movement in the NBA." http://www.bleacherrreport.com cited 16 April 2014.
"Summer Forecast: When Will the NBA Expand?" http://www.sports.espn.go.com cited 3 August 2009.
"Teams." http://www.basketball-reference.com cited 5 February 2014.
———. http://www.sportsencyclopdia.com cited 12 February 2014.
"The NBA's Growing Global Appeal." http://www.sportsbusinessnews.com cited 17 November 2005.
Thomsen, Ian. "NBA Mulling Idea of Five-Team Expansion in Europe." http://www.si.com cited 3 August 2009.
Washburn, Gary. "NBA Owners Cool to Expansion." http://www.seattlepi.com cited 3 August 2009.
Woodson, Cleve. "Ex-Bobcats Owner Blasts Charlotte." http://www.wcnc.com cited 23 February 2014.

Media Guides

Official NBA Guide: 2013–14 Edition (New York, NY: NBA Properties, 2013).
Official NBA Register: 2013–14 Edition (New York, NY: NBA Properties, 2013).

Index

F.P. Jozsa Jr., *National Basketball Association Strategies*,
SpringerBriefs in Economics 84, DOI 10.1007/978-3-319-10058-6

MIX
Papier aus verantwortungsvollen Quellen
Paper from responsible sources
FSC® C105338

If you have any concerns about our products,
you can contact us on
ProductSafety@springernature.com

In case Publisher is established outside the EU,
the EU authorized representative is:
Springer Nature Customer Service Center GmbH
Europaplatz 3, 69115 Heidelberg, Germany

Printed by Libri Plureos GmbH
in Hamburg, Germany